PRICE GUIDE

TO

Collector's Encyclopedia of

OCCUPIED JAPAN

Series I–V

COLLECTOR BOOKS

A Division of Schroeder Publishing Co., Inc.

The current values in this book should be used only as a guide. They are not intended to set prices, which vary from one section of the country to another. Auction prices as well as dealer prices vary greatly and are affected by condition as well as demand. Neither the Author nor the Publisher assumes responsibility for any losses that might be incurred as a result of consulting this guide.

Searching For A Publisher?

We are always looking for knowledgeable people considered to be experts within their fields. If you feel that there is a real need for a book on your collectible subject and have a large comprehensive collection contact Collector Books.

On the Cover:
Uncle Sam, 4½", $35.00
Rams Head Planter, $15.00
Angel Watching Child, $30.00
Indian Condiment Set, $35.00
Two-sided Puzzle, $25.00
American Children "Little Astrologer," $125.00
"Praying" Girl Vase, $12.00
Compote, two-piece, 9½", "Andrea," $150.00
Kaleidoscope "3 Pigs," $25.00
Violin Boy Planter, $15.00

Additional copies of this book may be ordered from:

Collector Books
P.O. Box 3009
Paducah, KY 42002-3009
or
Gene Florence

P.O. Box 22186
Lexington, Kentucky 40522

P.O. Box 64
Astatula, Florida 34705

@ $9.95. Add $2.00 for postage and handling.

Printed by IMAGE GRAPHICS, INC., Paducah, Kentucky

Page 8

Top Row:

Dogs ....$3.50 – 4.50
Pigs ....$5.50 – 6.50
Lady Bugs ....$8.50 – 10.00
Ducks ....$3.50 – 3.75

2nd Row:

Dogs ....$7.00 – 8.50
Bird ....$3.50 – 4.00
Receiving Set ....$3.50 – 4.50

3rd Row:

Dogs ....$9.00 – 10.00
Deer ....$5.00 – 6.00
Duck ....$6.00 – 6.50
Bird ....$3.50 – 3.75

4th Row:

Dogs ....$8.00 – 9.50
Birds ....$3.00 – 3.50
Lamb ....$2.50 – 3.00
Turtle ....$8.00 – 10.00
Bee ....$8.00 – 10.00

5th Row:

Dogs ....$12.50 – 20.00

Page 10

Top Row:

Bears ....$7.00 – 7.50 ea.
Dogs ....$5.00 – 6.00
Monkey Group ....$4.50 – 5.00

2nd Row:

Dog (same dog as in top row, only larger)......$7.00 – 7.50
Horse ....$6.00 – 7.50
Pig ....$5.00 – 5.50
Peacocks ....$5.00 – 6.00
Mouse ....$8.00 – 10.00

3rd Row:

Cat ....$4.00 – 4.50
Cat Groups ....$8.00 – 10.00
Butterflies ....$7.50 – 8.50
Dog ....$3.00 – 3.50

4th Row:

Cats ....$5.00 – 5.50
Horse Drawn Planter ....$5.00 – 6.00
Ox Drawn Planter ....$4.50 – 5.00
Dogs ....$6.00 – 6.50

5th Row:

Frog Ash Tray ....$12.00 – 15.00
Frog Vase ....$15.00 – 20.00
Fish...$3.00 – 3.50
Peacock ....$5.00 – 6.50

Cat Pencil Holder ....$3.50 – 4.00

Page 12

Top Row:

Coal Bin and Tray ....$17.50 – 20.00
Elephant Set (5 Trays) ....$17.50 – 20.00

2nd Row:

Alligator ....$11.00 – 12.50
"Wedgwood" Types ....$8.00 – 10.00
Frog ....$12.00 – 15.00

3rd Row:

Dresser and Top ....$6.00 – 6.50
Cigarette Boxes (4 Trays) ....$17.50 – 22.50

4th Row:

Cigarette Box (4 Trays) ....$15.00 – 17.50
Ash Trays (part of sets above) ....$2.50 – 3.00

Bottom:

Square Ash Tray ....$2.00 – 2.50
Rose Ash Tray ....$2.50 – 3.00 ea.
    Set of 4 and Box ....$17.50 – 20.00
Negro Holder ....$22.50 – 25.00
Queen of Hearts, Part of Set ....$3.00 – 3.50 ea.
Oriental Face, Part of Set ....$3.00 – 3.50
    Set w/box ....$17.50 – 20.00
Leaf ....$3.00 – 3.50
Rectangular Tray ....$3.00 – 3.50

Page 14

Top Row:

Rotating Cable, Car, San Francisco ....$20.00 – 25.00
Horses, Lexington, Ky ....$5.00 – 6.00

2nd Row:

St. Louis Zoo....................................$3.00 – 4.00
Large Cowboy Tray ....$3.00 – 3.50
Hollywood...$3.00 – 4.00

3rd Row:

Dog Cigarette or Jewel Box ....$8.50 – 9.50
St. Petersburg, Fla. Tray ....$3.00 – 3.50
Jewel Box ....$6.00 – 6.50
Double Tray ....$3.50 – 4.50
Cowboy Boot Lighter/Tray ....$12.50 – 15.00

4th Row:

Large Ash Tray ....$4.50 – 5.00
Small Tray ....$2.50 – 3.00
Devil Ash Tray ....$12.50 – 15.00

Bottom:

Silent butler ....$10.00 – 12.50
Butter Dish (Glass Liner) ....$10.00 – 12.50
Florida Ash Tray ....$2.50 – 3.00
Cigarette Box/Ash Tray on Stand .....$15.00 – 20.00

Page 16

Top Row:

Cream Pitcher (Part of Tea Set)......................................$9.00 – 10.00
Egg Cup (Part of Dinnerware Set)..............................$12.50 – 15.00
Pitcher ....$5.00 – 6.00
Half Potty ....$3.00 – 3.50

2nd Row:

Book Ends...$20.00 – 25.00 pr.
Pitcher ....$10.00 – 12.00

3rd Row:

Stacking Set (missing one part and lid)......................$3.00 ea./12.50 set
Black Boy at Outhouse ....$22.50 – 25.00
Cup and Saucer ....$17.50 – 20.00
Dutch Girl Bell..$17.50 – 20.00
Candle Holder ....$17.50 ea./35.00 pr.

Bottom:

Cornucopia Vase...$4.50 – 5.00
Vase..$4.00 – 4.50
Covered Powder Jar ....$8.00 – 10.00
Butt Snuffer..$4.50 – 5.00
Pitcher and Vase ....$3.50 – 4.00

Page 18

Canisters ....$25.00 – 30.00 ea./150.00 – 180.00 set

Page 20

Top Row:

Dancers, Working Key Wind.....................................$35.00 – 40.00
    Non Working ....$12.50 – 15.00
Reindeer ....$10.00 – 12.50
Baby Rattle...$17.50 – 20.00

2nd Row:

Baby Rattle..$17.50 – 20.00
Dog...$10.00 – 12.50
Doll, Movable Legs ....$22.50 – 25.00

3rd Row:

Pig (Tape Measure)..$17.50 – 20.00
Doll (Bisque-Like) ....$15.00 – 17.50
Scotty Dog, Working Key Wind...................................$35.00 – 40.00
    Non Working ....$12.50 – 15.00

Bottom:

Composition Doll...$17.50 – 20.00
Negro Doll, Mint w/Clothes ....$40.00 – 45.00
    As Pictured ....$15.00 – 20.00
12" Doll, Mint ....$35.00 – 40.00
    Some Damage ....$15.00 – 20.00
5" Doll, Mint ....$20.00 – 25.00
    Some damage, as shown ....$10.00 – 12.50
Football Player ....$12.50 – 15.00

Page 22

Place Settings:

Two ....$25.00 – 35.00
Three ....$35.00 – 50.00
Four ....$50.00 – 75.00

Four w/Tureen and Platter ....$100.00 – 125.00
Five ....$110.00 – 135.00
Six ....$150.00 – 200.00

Page 24

Top Row:

Cup (Saucer?)...$6.00 – 6.50
Demi/Set ....$10.00 – 12.50
Cherry China Sets ....$8.00 – 12.00
Hexagonal Demitasse Set ....$10.00 – 12.00

2nd Row:

1st and 4th Sets ....$6.00 – 7.50
2nd and 5th Demitasse Sets ....$10.00 – 12.00
Middle Set ....$15.00 – 17.50

3rd Row:

1st and 2nd Sets ....$10.00 – 12.00
3rd and 4th Sets ....$15.00 – 17.50
5th Cup only..$12.50 – 15.00

4th Row:

1st Demitasse Set ....$12.50 – 15.00
2nd and 4th Sets ....$10.00 – 12.00
Middle Set ....$15.00 – 20.00
5th Demitasse Set...$5.00 – 6.00

5th Row:

1st Set ....$12.00 – 15.00
2nd and 4th Sets ....$12.00 – 15.00
Middle Set ....$20.00 – 25.00
5th Set, Souvenir Santa Claus, Ind...............................$12.50 – 15.00

Page 26

Top Row:

Plate "Noritake" ....$10.00 – 12.00

2nd Row:

Hexagonal Plate ....$3.00 – 3.50
2nd and 4th Plates ....$3.00 – 3.50
3rd Plate ....$8.00 – 10.00
5th Plate ....$2.00 – 2.50

3rd Row:

Plate, Souvenir of Oklahoma City, Okla. ....$4.00 – 5.00
2nd Plate w/Sailboat ....$8.00 – 10.00
Ohio Map ....$15.00 – 17.50
Celery...$5.00 – 6.00

4th Row:

Violet Plate...$15.00 – 17.50
Fruit Plate ....$12.50 – 15.00
Flower Plate ....$10.00 – 12.50

Bottom:

1st Plate ....$2.00 – 2.50
Bonbon Tray ....$8.50 – 10.00
Flower Plate ....$7.50 – 9.00

Page 28

Cherry China, 8 Place Setting w/Serving Pieces .....$200.00 – 300.00

12 Place Setting with Serving Pieces...................$250.00 – 400.00
Noritake China, 8 Place Setting w/Serving Pieces ..$250.00 – 350.00
12 Place Setting with Serving Pieces...................$300.00 – 500.00

Page 30

Top Row:
Ship ....$9.00 – 10.00
Bisque Boy and Girl..............................$17.50 – 22.50
Castle...$6.00 – 7.00
Bisque Boy..$15.00 – 17.50

2nd Row:
Castle...$4.00 – 5.00
Cats ....$20.00 – 22.00
Goldfish..$8.00 – 10.00
Bisque Boy and Girl..............................$12.50 – 15.00

Bottom:
Castle atop Bridge..................................$8.00 – 10.00
Pagoda Bridge......................................$10.00 – 12.00
Mermaid..$20.00 – 22.00

Page 32

Top Row:
Blue Cologne and Tray ....$22.50 – 27.50/11.00 – 13.50 ea.

2nd Row:
Perfume...$17.50
w/atomizer..$30.00
Duck, w/Sticker......................................$6.50 – 7.50
Pink Cologne or Perfume.......................$17.50 – 20.00

3rd Row:
Shakers..$17.50 – 20.00 pr.
Dogs, w/Sticker ....$30.00 – 32.50 set
Shakers, w/Stand ....$20.00 – 25.00 pr.

4th Row:
Sport Glasses...$30.00 – 40.00
w/case...$40.00 – 50.00
Ash Tray..$15.00 – 20.00

Page 34

Lacquerware Lamp ....$50.00 – 75.00
Colonial Single......................................$30.00 – 35.00
Colonial Single, sans Socket.................$30.00 – 40.00
w/socket..$40.00 – 50.00
Colonial Pair, Left.................................$75.00 – 90.00
Pair Lamps, Right ....$75.00 – 90.00

Page 36

Plates...$4.50 – 5.00
Coasters, 2 Sizes.....................................$2.50 – 3.00
Wall Shelf Unit ....$40.00 – 50.00
Lamp Base ....$50.00 – 75.00
Ice Bucket and Tongs.............................$35.00 – 50.00
Salad Bowl w/Fork and Spoon ....$30.00 – 40.00
Bowl w/6 Individual Bowls and Spoon ....$40.00 – 50.00

Page 38

Top Row:
Lamp Lighter ....$17.50 – 20.00

Donkey Lighter ....$20.00 – 22.50
Boot Lighter ....$7.50 – 8.50

2nd Row:
Coat of Armor Lighter ....$15.00 – 17.50
Inlaid Lighter ....$12.50 – 15.00
Mint Compote ....$5.00 – 6.00
Table Gun Lighter ....$20.00 – 22.50
Shoe Pin Cushion ....$7.50 – 8.00

3rd Row:
Table Lighter..$5.00 – 6.00
Gun Lighter ....$12.00 – 13.50
Bulldog Pencil Sharpener ....$10.00 – 12.00
Shaker and Mustard Set w/Tray............$22.50 – 25.00
Trophies ....$2.00 – 2.50
Donkey Jewel Chest...............................$17.50 – 20.00

Bottom:
Tea Holder ....$15.00 – 18.00
Nut Dish ....$5.00 – 6.00
Key Lighter ....$12.00 – 15.00
Pencil Lighter..$25.00 – 30.00

Page 40

Top Row:
All Items Save 2nd Teapot........................$4.00 – 5.00
2nd Teapot w/Removable Lid.....................$6.00 – 7.50

2nd Row:
All Items Save Half Potty and Lookout Mt. Pitcher........$3.50 – 4.00
Half Potty ....$3.00 – 3.50
Lookout Mt. Pitcher..................................$4.00 – 5.00

3rd Row:
All Items Save Martha/George and Floral Vase ....$2.50 – 3.00
Martha and George Set ....$15.00 – 17.50
Blue Floral Vase ....$7.50 – 9.00

4th Row:
All items ....$4.00 – 5.00

5th Row:
All Items Save Small Trays and Nude Boy ....$3.50 – 4.00
Nude Boy ....$4.50 – 5.00
Tray w/6 Pieces—Only the trays are marked "Made in Occupied Japan"
Removable Lid on Pitcher ....$17.50 – 20.00 (complete)
Incomplete...$2.00 each piece

Page 42

Large Umbrella, approx. 3 ft. across........$25.00 – 30.00
Wood Jewelry Box..................................$12.50 – 15.00
Camera, Self Developing Film ....$100.00 – 150.00
Decorative Fan ....$2.00 – 3.00
Small Umbrellas......................................$2.00 – 3.00
Christmas Ornament ....$12.50 – 15.00
Doll Chest..$25.00 – 30.00
Box, Secret Opening ....$25.00 – 30.00
Ship (String and Wood) ....$10.00 – 12.00
Santa on Sleigh ....$45.00 – 50.00
Rag Time Band, Boxed Set ....$25.00 – 30.00 ($4.00 ea)

Page 44

Top Row:

All Items Save Bee..$5.00 – 6.00

Bee...$6.50 – 7.50

2nd Row:

All Items Save Rabbit...$5.50 – 7.00

Rabbit...$7.50 – 9.00

3rd Row:

All Items..$5.00 – 6.50

4th Row:

Duck and Donkey ....$5.50 – 6.50

Boat...$15.00 – 17.50

5th Row:

Donkey, Left ....$10.00 – 12.00

Donkey, Center ....$8.00 – 10.00

Zebra ....$8.00 – 10.00

Page 46

Top Row:

Small Girl...$3.50 – 4.00

Oriental Heads ....$30.00 – 40.00

2nd Row:

1st and 4th Planters ....$7.50 – 10.00

2nd and 3rd Planters/Bookends ....$17.50 – 20.00

3rd Row:

All Items...$7.50 – 10.00

4th Row:

All Items Save Center Pieces.........................$8.00 – 10.00

Tall Center Pieces ....$15.00 – 17.50

Page 48

Top Row:

All Items Save Windmills Miniature Toby Shakers ....$12.00 – 15.00 pr.

Windmills and Toby ....$15.00 – 17.50 pr.

2nd Row:

All items Save Martha and George ....$12.00 – 15.00 pr.

Martha and George ....$20.00 – 25.00 pr.

3rd Row:

All Items Save Frogs and Rabbits.................$10.00 – 12.00 pr.

Frogs and Rabbits ....$20.00 – 25.00 pr.

4th Row:

Three Piece Sets ....$20.00 – 25.00

5th Row:

Three Piece Sets, Save Cucumbers.............$20.00 – 25.00

Cucumbers ....$25.00 – 30.00

Page 50

Top Row:

Chicken and Girl..$7.50 – 8.00 ea.

Boats /3 Piece Sets...$17.50 – 20.00

    Gaily Decorated ....$20.00 – 25.00

2nd Row:

4 Piece Metal Set ....$20.00 – 22.50

Glass Shakers and Metal Stand....................$20.00 – 25.00

Hobnail Shakers ....$17.50 – 20.00 pr.

Frogs/3 Piece Set..$20.00 – 25.00

Clown ....$12.00 – 15.00

3rd Row:

Tomato, Pr..$8.00 – 10.00

Tomato Sets on Leaf w/Mustard....................$20.00 – 25.00

4th Row:

Blue/White Shakers ....$20.00 – 25.00 pr.

   (Match egg cup on page 17)

Windmills w/Moving Blades ....$25.00 – 30.00 pr.

Negro Cooks, pr..$40.00 – 50.00 pr.

Cottages and Peppers ....$10.00 – 12.00

Boy...$7.50 – 8.00

5th Row:

Beehive Set ....$25.00 – 30.00

Beehive Sugar and Marmalade ....$20.00 – 25.00

Separate Sugar ....$10.00 – 12.50

Ceramic Set on Tray ....$20.00 – 25.00

Page 52

Top Row:

Statue, Flat Gap, Ky.......................................$20.00 – 25.50

Pitcher, Lookout Mt., Tenn..............................$4.00 – 5.00

Statue, Canadian National Exhibition.........$12.00 – 15.00

2nd Row:

Toothpick, Wisconsin ....$5.00 – 5.50

Cats, Niagara Falls, Canada ....$8.00 – 10.00

Plate, Oklahoma City, Okla. ....$3.25 – 4.00

Vase, Canada..$5.00 – 6.00

Cup and Saucer, Santa Claus, Ind..............$12.50 – 15.00

Pitchers, Mt. Vernon, Va. ....$15.00 – 17.00 pr.

3rd Row:

Tray, New York City ....$2.50 – 3.00

Tray, St. Louis Zoo ....$2.50 – 3.00

Tray, Catskill Mts. ....$2.50 – 3.00

4th Row:

Ash Tray, Lexington, Ky. ....$5.00 – 6.00

Map Dish, Ohio or Other States....................$15.00 – 17.50

Ash Tray, San Francisco ....$20.00 – 25.00

Page 54

Top Row:

Sugar, Left...$15.00 – 17.50

Teapot, Sugar, and Creamer........................$85.00 – 100.00

Individual Teapot ....$15.00 – 17.50

2nd Row:

As Shown ....$100.00 – 150.00

3rd Row:

Creamer and Sugar ....$15.00 – 17.50

Teapot ....$17.50 – 20.00

Page 56

Top Row:
Tea Set ....$60.00 – 75.00

Middle:
Bowl...$25.00 – 35.00
Square Flat Dish..$15.00 – 18.00

Bottom:
Cup and Saucer Set w/Stand ....$75.00 – 100.00
Candy Dish...$15.00 – 17.50

Page 58

Top Row:
All Toby Mugs ....$15.00 – 17.50

2nd Row:
All Toby Mugs Save 3rd from Left ....$15.00 – 20.00
3rd Toby Mug from Left................................$20.00 – 25.00

3rd Row:
Tobies, either end.......................................$25.00 – 30.00
Other Toby Mugs...$15.00 – 17.50

4th Row:
Large Heads ....$30.00 – 40.00
Small Heads ....$20.00 – 25.00

5th Row:
1st Two Toby Mugs......................................$12.50 – 15.00
3rd Toby..$30.00 – 35.00
Barrel Mug..$15.00 – 20.00
MacArthur Toby ....$65.00 – 75.00

Page 60

Top Row:
All Items..$5.00 – 6.00

2nd Row:
All Items Save Topless Girl.........................$5.00 – 7.00
Topless Girl...$10.00 – 12.00

3rd Row:
All Items Save Naked Girl and Wagon..........$3.50 – 5.00
Naked Girl and Vase....................................$10.00 – 12.00
Girl w/Wagon...$12.00 – 15.00

4th Row:
All Items Save Angel on Star.......................$5.00 – 8.00
Angel on Shooting Star................................$10.00 – 12.00

5th Row:
All Items, Save Tree ....$8.00 – 10.00
Tree ....$4.50 – 5.00

Page 62

Top Row:
Dancing Elephant in Original Box..............$75.00 – 100.00
Dancing Bear in Original Box ....$50.00 – 65.00
Hopping Squirrel..$50.00 – 75.00

2nd Row:
Running Mouse in Original Box...................$35.00 – 50.00

Wind-Up Car..$100.00 – 125.00
Baby Jeep in Box ....$75.00 – 100.00

3rd Row:
Car w/Box ....$100.00 – 125.00
Fly Pin on Card ....$4.50 – 5.00
Beetle ....$30.00 – 40.00
Watches on Card...$10.00 – 15.00 ea.

Bottom:
Box of Puzzles w/Instructions ....$75.00 – 100.00

Page 64

Top Row (Left to Right):
All Vases, Save 5th and 6th ....$4.00 – 6.00 ea.
5th Vase, looks like Egyptian Hieroglyphics.................$8.00 – 10.00
6th, Kutani-Type..$6.00 – 8.00

2nd Row:
All Save 4th Pair ....$8.00 – 10.00 pr.
4th Pair, Kutani-type....................................$14.00 – 18.00 pr.

3rd Row:
Six Kutani-types..$6.00 – 8.00
2nd Vase (unusual shape) ....$8.00 – 10.00
6th, 7th, 8th Vases......................................$5.00 – 6.00 ea.

4th Row:
Six Kutani-types..$6.00 – 8.00 ea.
Others ....$3.00 – 4.00 ea.

Bottom:
All Vases...$3.00 – 5.00 ea.

Page 66

Top Row:
All Vases...$5.00 – 8.00 ea.

2nd Row:
All Vases Save 2nd and 5th ....$7.00 – 8.00 ea.
2nd Vase, Children......................................$10.00 – 12.00
5th Vase, Seated Figure ....$20.00 – 25.00

3rd Row:
All Vases Save George Washington ....$6.00 – 8.00
George Washington ....$10.00 – 12.00

Bottom:
1st Vase, fine quality...................................$30.00 – 35.00
Iris Vases..$50.00 – 60.00 ea.
4th Vase, enclosed figure ....$30.00 – 40.00
5th Vase ....$12.50 – 15.00

Page 68

Top Row:
Elf on Praying Mantis ....$25.00 – 30.00
Angel..$5.00 – 7.00

Middle:
Seated Elves with Planters ....$15.00 – 20.00
Angel w/Flute...$8.00 – 10.00

Bottom:
Seated Elf ....$12.50 – 15.00

Reclining Elf ....$12.50 – 15.00
Angel w/Sleeping Child.............................$40.00 – 50.00
Standing Angel..$8.00 – 10.00

Page 70

Top Row:
Peasant Girl Standing................................$20.00 – 25.00
Farmer w/Rake...$25.00 – 35.00
M'Lady w/Dove.......................................$100.00 – 125.00
Peasant Boy..$25.00 – 30.00
Seated Girl ....$25.00 – 30.00

Middle:
Man w/Cane ....$20.00 – 30.00
Boy w/Dog ....$25.00 – 35.00

Bottom:
Boy Holding Mug ....$25.00 – 30.00
Standing Lay w/Hat ....$20.00 – 22.50
Lad w/Cloak ....$20.00 – 22.50
Seated Little Boy..$15.00 – 17.50
Standing Dowager.......................................$17.50 – 20.00
Peasant Lass ....$12.50 – 15.00
M'Lord Standing...$35.00 – 50.00

Page 72

Top Row:
Boy and Girl Pair ....$100.00 – 125.00

2nd Row:
Seated Musician Pair..................................$60.00 – 70.00
Plaques Pair, Mint......................................$45.00 – 50.00
Boys Holding Leaves ....$40.00 – 50.00 ea.

3rd and 4th Row:
Girl and Boy on Left Pair...........................$50.00 – 60.00
Seated Boy and Girl ....$17.50 – 22.50
Japanese Pair..$30.00 – 40.00
Man and Woman on Right Pair....................$50.00 – 60.00

Bottom:
All Seated Figures ....$15.00 – 17.50

Page 74

Top Row:
All Items Save Center Boy w/Duck...............$7.50 – 10.00
Boy w/Duck ....$12.50 – 15.00

2nd Row:
All Items Save Reclining Girl.......................$6.00 – 8.00
Reclining Girl w/Bird ....$10.00 – 12.00

3rd Row:
All items..$5.00 – 6.00

4th Row:
1st Five Items ....$5.00 – 6.00

Last Five Items...$15.00 – 20.00

5th Row:
Boy and Dog, Left.......................................$20.00 – 25.00

Remaining Items ....$20.00 – 22.50

Page 76

Top Row:
All Items Save Clarinet Player & Drummer....................$6.00 – 8.00
Clarinet Player and Bisque Drummer ....$12.50 – 17.50

Middle:
All Items Save Small Figure in Front ....$10.00 – 12.00
Small Figure (Gabriel?) ....$4.00 – 5.50

Bottom:
All Items Save Last ....$6.00 – 8.00
Last Boy and Dog ....$17.50 – 20.00

Page 78

Top Row:
Shelf Sitters...$15.00 – 17.50
Boy and Girl at Ends....................................$6.00 – 8.00
Middle Two Girls ....$15.00 – 20.00

Middle:
Shelf Sitters...$15.00 – 17.50
Boy and Girl in Center.................................$6.00 – 8.00
Girl in White ....$4.00 – 5.00

Bottom:
Shelf Sitters...$15.00 – 17.50
Tall Girl, Small Girl....................................$10.00 – 12.00

Page 80

Top Row:
Ballerina..$40.00 – 45.00
White Dress Dancer ....$15.00 – 17.50
Pink Dress Dancer......................................$10.00 – 12.50
Lavender Dress Dancer...............................$25.00 – 30.00

Middle:
Girl Ballerina and Green Dress Dancer ....$10.00 – 12.00
Tall Girl w/Hat...$25.00 – 30.00

Bottom:
All Dancers ....$9.00 – 10.00

Page 82

Top Row:
Boy and Girl...$20.00 – 25.00

2nd Row:
Colonial Man and Woman, Both Pairs ....$25.00 – 30.00
Pair, middle left...$12.00 – 15.00
Center Pair ....$9.00 – 10.00
Pair, middle right ....$15.00 – 20.00

Bottom:
Taller Couple ....$27.50 – 30.00
Center Pair ....$15.00 – 20.00
Couple at Right ....$20.00 – 25.00

Page 84

Top Row:
Lady Holding Hat ....$25.00 – 30.00

Dutch Sailor w/Bag..$17.50 – 20.00

Middle:
Lady w/Feathered Hat..$25.00 – 30.00
Lady Holding Hat ....$25.00 – 30.00

Bottom:
M'Lady w/Basket...$30.00 – 35.00
Dutch Girl ....$20.00 – 25.00
Windmill Shakers..$12.50 – 15.00
Windmill Shakers w/Turning Blades.........................$25.00 – 30.00

Page 86

Top Row (Left to Right):
1st, 2nd, 4th, and 7th Couple ....$12.50 – 15.00
3rd Couple...$5.00 – 6.00
5th Couple...$4.50 – 5.00
6th Group ....$17.50 – 20.00

2nd Row:
1st, 2nd, and 7th Couple ....$12.50 – 15.00
3rd, 5th, and 6th Couple...$5.50 – 6.50
4th, Bride and Groom ....$27.50 – 30.00

3rd Row:
All Couples Save 6th ....$12.50 – 15.00
6th Couple...$5.50 – 6.00

4th Row:
1st Couple, fine detail ....$22.50 – 25.00
2nd and 5th Couples...$12.50 – 15.00
6th Couple, Canadian National Exposition Souvenir ..$12.00 – 14.00
3rd Couple...$10.00 – 12.00
Bride and Groom ....$35.00 – 40.00
7th Couple...$15.00 – 17.50

5th Row:
Man Pushing Sleigh ....$75.00 – 100.00
2nd Couple...$30.00 – 35.00
3rd Couple...$35.00 – 40.00
4th Couple...$20.00 – 25.00

Page 88

Top Row:
1st, 2nd, and 5th Musicians.......................................$5.50 – 6.50 ea.
3rd Figure ....$15.00 – 18.00
4th Figure ....$8.00 – 10.00

2nd Row:
1st Figure ....$6.00 – 8.00
2nd Figure ....$3.00 – 3.50
3rd Pair, 5th Figure ....$10.00 – 12.00
4th Figure ....$3.50 – 4.00

3rd Row:
1st and 2nd Figures ....$5.00 – 6.00
Girl and Piano ....$15.00 – 17.50
Piano Ensemble...$37.50 – 40.00
Man and Piano ....$17.50 – 20.00

4th Row:
Seated Bisque Pair ....$60.00 – 75.00

Organ Grinders..$20.00 – 25.00
4th Man w/Fiddle...$12.50 – 15.00
6th and 7th Foursome...$30.00 – 35.00 pr.

5th Row:
Maid w/Suitor ....$22.50 – 25.00 pr.
3rd and 4th, Men ....$12.50 – 15.00
Seated Flutist ....$15.00 – 17.50
End Pair Musicians ....$30.00 – 35.00

Page 90

Top Row:
Figures 1, 3, 5, and 6...$7.00 – 9.00
Bisque Figures 2 and 8, Reclining Figure...................$10.00 – 12.00
Girl #7 ....$6.00 – 6.50

2nd Row:
Figures 1 and 4 ....$6.00 – 7.50
Rickshaw..$22.50 – 25.00
Man w/Clay Pots...$9.00 – 11.00
Shelf Sitter ....$15.00 – 17.50

3rd Row:
Shelf Sitters ....$15.00 – 17.50
Figures 2, 3, 4, 5, and 9...$6.00 – 7.50
Figure 6 ....$4.00 – 5.00
Bisque Girl #7 ....$12.50 – 15.00

4th Row:
Girls 1 and 7, fine detail...$20.00 – 22.50
Figures 2, 5, and 6..$15.00 – 20.00
3rd Figure ....$20.00 – 25.00
Tall Figure #4...$40.00 – 50.00

Page 92

Top Row:
Shelf Sitter ....$15.00 – 17.50
Figures 2 and 3...$8.00 – 10.00 ea.
Figures 4, 7, and 8 ....$4.50 – 6.00
Incense Burners...$14.00 – 16.00 ea.

2nd Row:
Figures 1, 2, 3...$8.00 – 10.00 ea.
Figures 4 and 5, Pair...$20.00 – 25.00
Figures 6 and 7 ....$6.00 – 7.00 ea.

3rd Row:
Rickshaw..$22.50 – 25.00
Bookends..$20.00 – 25.00 pr.
Figures 4 and 5, Pair ....$7.00 – 8.00

Bottom:
Pair, Each End..$25.00 – 30.00
Figures 3 and 4...$15.00 – 17.50 ea.
Figures 5 and 6, Pair ....$50.00 – 60.00

Page 94

Top Row:
1st Pair ....$3.50 – 4.00
Pairs 2 and 5 ....$7.50 – 9.50
3rd Pair ....$12.00 – 14.00
4th Pair ....$25.00 – 30.00

6th Pair ....$7.50 – 8.00

2nd Row:
Pairs 1 and 5 ....$20.00 – 25.00
Pairs 2 and 3 ....$15.00 – 18.00
4th Pair ....$12.50 – 15.00

3rd Row:
1st Figure ....$10.00 – 12.00
2nd Figure ....$10.00 – 12.00
Pairs 3 and 4 ....$30.00 – 35.00 pr.
Pairs 5 and 6 ....$10.00 – 12.50 pr.

4th Row:
Pairs 1 and 3, nice detail ....$60.00 – 70.00 pr.
2nd Pair, Signed Andrea ....$100.00 – 125.00 pr.

Page 96

Top Row:
Baseball Player..$8.00 – 10.00 ea.
Dwarfs, Bisque-like ....$10.00 – 12.00

2nd Row:
Musicians (two of set of six)..........................$6.00 – 8.00 ea.
Figures 2, 3, 4..$8.00 – 10.00 ea.

3rd Row:
Cherub Musicians, Bisque-like......................$10.00 – 12.50 ea.

4th Row:
Baseball Bears (Pink, Blue, Green Colors).....................$7.00 – 7.50 ea.
   Set: Pitcher, Batter, Catcher, and Spectator
Cherub Musician Bud Vases...........................$7.00 – 8.00 ea.

5th Row:
Elves, Sets of 6 or 8 Planter Backs ....$15.00 – 20.00 ea.
Sans Planters ....$15.00 – 20.00 ea.

Page 98

Top Row:
Ladies ....$7.50 – 10.00

2nd Row:
Lady w/Parasol ....$8.00 – 10.00
Boy w/Bag ....$9.00 – 10.00
Old Woman w/Balloons...................................$30.00 – 35.00
Bullfighter ....$8.00 – 10.00
Boy, Gold and White ....$12.00 – 15.00

Bottom:
Lady w/Basket ....$10.00 – 12.00
Colonial Man ....$6.00 – 7.00
Last Two Ladies...$6.00 – 8.00

Page 100

Top Row:
All ....$6.00 – 8.00

2nd Row:
1st and 5th Ladies ....$6.00 – 8.00
2nd Lady ....$5.00 – 6.00
3rd and 4th ....$8.00 – 10.00
6th Lady with left column..............................$6.00 – 7.00

3rd Row:
All ....$6.00 – 8.00

4th Row:
1st Lady Seated ....$4.00 – 5.00
2nd and 4th Seated Men..................................$8.00 – 10.00
3rd Man ....$6.00 – 8.00
5th Lady ....$4.00 – 5.00

Page 102

Top Row:
1st, 4th, 6th...$8.00 – 10.00 ea.
2nd and 5th Lady ....$12.00 – 15.00
3rd Seated Man ....$17.50 – 20.00

Middle:
1st Lady..$8.00 – 10.00
2nd Seated Lady ....$12.00 – 15.00
3rd Lady w/Dog ....$10.00 – 12.00

Bottom:
1st Gal ....$12.50 – 15.00
Men ....$10.00 – 15.00 ea.
3rd and 5th Ladies ....$15.00 – 20.00

Page 104

Top Row:
Small Turbaned Boy ....$6.00 – 7.00
Large Turbaned Boy ....$15.00 – 17.50
Hula Dancer ....$10.00 – 12.00

2nd Row:
Canadian Policeman...$15.00 – 20.00
Uncle Sam ....$30.00 – 35.00
Large Cowboy ....$12.50 – 15.00
Small Cowboy..$10.00 – 12.00

3rd Row:
Matador ....$8.00 – 10.00
Cowgirl ....$12.50 – 15.00
Incense Burners..$14.00 – 16.00 ea.
Cowgirl, Right..$10.00 – 12.00

4th Row:
Indian ....$12.50 – 15.00
Indian in Canoe ....$5.00 – 6.00
Cowgirl ....$12.50 – 15.00
Indian Incense Burner......................................$18.00 – 20.00

Page 106

Clock ....$500.00 – 600.00

Page 6

Top Row:
Chickens Pr ....$20.00 – 22.50
Dog...$12.50 – 15.00
Woebegone Horse ....$10.00 – 12.50

2nd Row:
1st Dog, 7" ....$12.50 – 15.00
2nd and 3rd Dogs ....$12.50 – 15.00 ea.
Elephant ....$10.00 – 12.00
Bird...$12.00 – 15.00

3rd Row:
Frogs ....$15.00 – 17.50 ea.
Dog..$8.00 – 10.00
Cat on Bed/Set ....$15.00 – 17.50
Lamb ....$6.00 – 7.00

4th Row:
Frog ....$10.00 – 12.00
Dog/Set (3)...$10.00 – 12.50
Rabbit/Set (4) Dated ....$20.00 – 25.00

5th Row:
Bees ....$8.50 – 10.00 ea.
Elephants on Wood Set....................................$20.00 – 25.00
Cat ....$4.00 – 5.00
Cat (Black Celluloid) ....$10.00 – 12.00
Scotties (Celluloid) ....$8.00 – 10.00

Page 8

Top Row:
Dogs ....$15.00 – 20.00 ea.
Bird...$15.00 – 17.50
Frog (Bisque) ....$20.00 – 22.00

2nd Row:
Birds...$7.50 – 9.00 ea.
Dog...$10.00 – 12.00
Geese (Blue Base, Set 3).................................$17.50 – 20.00
Goose Pruning Feathers ....$6.00 – 7.00

3rd Row:
Bird ....$2.00 – 3.00
Dog (Rubber/Scottie) ....$8.00 – 10.00
Dog and Hydrant...$10.00 – 12.50
Penguin ....$7.00 – 8.00
Dog with Ribbon..$7.00 – 8.00

4th Row:
Dogs (First Three)...$6.00 – 7.50 ea.
Dog (Gray Dachshund) ....$12.00 – 15.00
Dog (Celluloid) ....$5.00 – 7.00

5th Row:
Bird ....$3.00 – 4.00
Swan ....$3.00 – 4.00
Monkey ....$4.00 – 5.00

Deer...$5.00 – 6.00
Duck (Humanoid) ....$15.00 – 20.00

Page 10

Top Row:
Cigarette Box and Tray ....$17.50 – 20.00
Coal Scuttle and Tray......................................$20.00 – 22.50

2nd Row:
Pirate Snuffer ....$9.00 – 10.00
Man with Fly on Nose.....................................$17.50 – 20.00
Kentucky Map...$12.00 – 15.00

3rd Row:
Frog on Lily Pad ....$12.50 – 14.00
Elephants with Trays.......................................$20.00 – 22.00
"Wedgwood-Like" Tray ....$10.00 – 12.50
Fish...$3.00 – 5.00
Bridge Set...$3.00 – 3.50 ea.

Page 12

Top Row:
Sugar and Creamer on a Tray ....$15.00 – 20.00
Cowboy Hat Ash Tray (5" Width)...................$8.00 – 10.00
Candlestick, Pair ....$15.00 – 20.00
Tumbler (5 oz.) ....$6.00 – 7.50

2nd Row:
Desk Set (Exceptional Quality) ....$25.00 – 30.00
Match or Cigarette Holders.............................$3.00 – 5.00 ea.

3rd Row:
Piano Jewelry Holder......................................$15.00 – 17.50
Candy Container (Handled) ....$12.00 – 15.00
Antimony Desk Set ....$25.00 – 30.00

4th Row:
Ash Tray..$3.00 – 3.50
Ash Tray, Souvenir of Alaska..........................$5.00 – 6.00

Page 14

Top Row:
Dragon Mug ("Engraved "Sue").....................$15.00 – 20.00
Cigarette Holder..$3.00 – 4.00
Tea or Spice Canister.......................................$12.50 – 15.00

2nd Row:
Leaf Candy Dish ....$10.00 – 12.00
Salt & Pepper Shakers ....$8.00 – 10.00 pr.
Salt & Pepper Shakers on Tray ....$10.00 – 12.00
Open Candy Dish ....$6.00 – 8.00
Piano Cigarette Dispenser...............................$20.00 – 25.00

3rd Row:
Jewelry Boxes, 5 Assorted Sizes ....$10.00 – 15.00 ea.
Open Candy Dish...$10.00 – 12.00
Hand Warmer & Chamois Bag........................$25.00 – 30.00
Butter Dish..$12.50 – 15.00

Sugar & Creamer, Pair ....$12.50 – 15.00

4th Row:
Cowboy Ash Tray ....$3.50 – 5.00
Heart Ash Tray (Hot Springs, Ark.)..............$4.00 – 5.00
Cowboy Hat Ash Tray (3" Wide) ....$5.00 – 6.00

Page 16

Top Row:
Red Haired Doll ....$50.00 – 60.00
Blue Dressed Doll...$35.00 – 40.00
Japanese Set of Dolls in Box ....$75.00 – 100.00

2nd Row:
Football Player Doll.....................................$12.00 – 15.00
Baseball Players ....$15.00 – 20.00 ea.
Doll in White Gown.....................................$40.00 – 50.00

3rd Row:
Pink Teddy Bear ....$20.00 – 25.00
Doll in Blue (3" Composition).....................$30.00 – 35.00
Cat, Dog, Camel.......................................$9.00 – 10.00 ea.

Page 18

Top Row:
Mechanical Santa and Reindeer...............$100.00 – 125.00
Football Pin...$7.00 – 7.50
Rudolph, 7"...$15.00 – 20.00
Small Reindeer..$7.50 – 8.50

2nd Row:
Rickshaw..$12.00 – 15.00
Mechanical Santa ....$50.00 – 65.00

3rd Row:
Stagecoaches ....$12.00 – 15.00 ea.
Goggles ....$7.50 – 10.00
Floating Water Lily...$8.50 – 10.00
Mechanical Scottie with Shoe....................$30.00 – 35.00
Christmas Ornaments in Box ....$17.50 – 20.00

Page 20

Tea Sets - Place Settings
Two ....$35.00 – 40.00
Three ....$45.00 – 50.00
Four ....$45.00 – 50.00
Four with Tureen and Platter ....$90.00 – 95.00
Five ....$100.00 – 115.00
Six ....$150.00 – 175.00
Tray, Sugar, Creamer, Teapot....................$25.00 – 30.00
Tray, Sugar, and Creamer ....$17.50 – 20.00
Bath Set, 3 Pieces.......................................$30.00 – 35.00

Page 22

Top Row:
1st and 5th Sets, Hexagonal ....$12.50 – 15.00 ea.
2nd Set ....$6.00 – 7.50
3rd and 4th Sets.......................................$7.00 – 8.50 ea.

2nd Row:
1st Cup Only ....$8.00 – 9.00
2nd Set ....$10.00 – 12.50

3rd Set ....$12.50 – 15.00
4th (Satsuma) Set..$22.50 – 25.00
5th Dragon Set ....$17.50 – 20.00

3rd Row:
1st, 3rd, 4th Sets....................................$10.00 – 12.50 ea.
2nd Set, Flower Petal ....$20.00 – 25.00
5th Set, Blue Willow ....$12.00 – 15.00

4th Row:
1st, 4th, 5th Sets....................................$12.50 – 15.00 ea.
2nd, 3rd Sets...$15.00 – 17.50 ea.

Page 24

Top Row:
Sweetmeat Set..$100.00 – 125.00
Clock ....$65.00 – 75.00

2nd Row:
Pastoral Scene Plate ....$75.00 – 100.00
Fall and Spring Plates ....$12.50 – 15.00 ea.
Square Plate ....$12.50 – 15.00

Page 26

Top Row:
Gold Decorated Plate ....$15.00 – 17.00
Pagoda Plate ....$12.00 – 13.50

2nd Row:
Scenic Plate ....$8.00 – 10.00
Octagonal Plate ....$10.00 – 12.50
Small Leaf Plate ....$3.50 – 4.50

3rd Row:
Square Bowl...$15.00 – 17.50
Plate with Ladies...$17.50 – 20.00
Maple Leaf Plate...$5.50 – 7.50
Japanese Scenic Plate.................................$17.50 – 20.00
Flowered Bowl ....$8.00 – 10.00

4th Row:
Small Star Shaped Items ....$4.00 – 5.50 ea.

Page 28

4 Place Setting w/Serving Pieces...........$175.00 – 200.00
6 Place Setting w/Serving Pieces...........$225.00 – 250.00
8 Place Setting w/Serving Pieces...........$275.00 – 300.00
12 Place Setting w/Serving Pieces.........$400.00 – 450.00

Page 34

"Blue Willow" Grill Plate..........................$12.50 – 15.00
"Blue Willow" Salad Plate............................$6.00 – 8.00
"Blue Willow" Platter..................................$30.00 – 40.00
"Old Willoware" cup and Saucer...............$20.00 – 22.50
"Gold Castle" Soup Bowl ....$6.00 – 8.00

Page 36

Top Row:
Blooming Flower ....$3.00 – 5.00

2nd Row:
Frog Hanger ....$17.50 – 20.00

Man Hanger ....$15.00 – 17.50
Mermaid..$15.00 – 17.50
Floating Water Lily.......................................$8.50 – 10.00

3rd Row:
Ship ....$7.50 – 9.00
Arches ....$10.00 – 12.50 ea.

Page 38
Top Row:
Wind Chimes ....$25.00 – 30.00

2nd Row:
Pink Cologne...$25.00 – 30.00
Small Animals with Sticker ....$7.00 – 9.00 ea.
Perfume Bottles......................................$20.00 – 25.00 ea.

3rd Row:
Perfume Bottles......................................$25.00 – 30.00 ea.
Salt & Pepper Shakers ....$12.50 – 15.00 pr.
Girl with Egg Timer ....$12.50 – 15.00

4th Row:
Toy Binoculars..$15.00 – 17.50
Perfume & Atomizer Set.............................$45.00 – 55.00
Perfume Bottle ....$25.00 – 30.00
Mustard & Lid...$15.00 – 17.50

Page 40
Top Row:
Tray, Five Part, Handled/Very Heavy ......$75.00 – 100.00
Wine Goblet ....$12.00 – 15.00

2nd Row:
Cup and Saucer, Sets............................$15.00 – 20.00 ea.
Bowl and Spoon (missing underplate)........$12.50 – 15.00

Page 42
Top Row:
Bisque Lamps, Paired ea.......................$60.00 – 75.00 ea.
    Pair ....$135.00 – 150.00
3rd Lamp ....$40.00 – 50.00

2nd Row:
Mary and Lamb..$75.00 – 100.00
"Wedgwood" Types................................$45.00 – 50.00 ea.

Page 44
Top Row:
Standing Colonial Couple.......................$35.00 – 40.00 ea.
    Pair ....$80.00 – 85.00
Seated Colonial Couple..........................$35.00 – 40.00 ea.
    Pair ....$80.00 – 95.00

2nd Row:
Oriental Dancer..$30.00 – 35.00
Colonial Lady..$20.00 – 25.00
Colonial Couple..$25.00 – 30.00
Lamp Base with Fish Inset.........................$25.00 – 30.00

Page 46
Top Row:
Telephone Cigarette Lighters...............$17.50 – 20.00 ea.

Cast Metal Skillet and Handle ....$15.00 – 20.00

2nd Row:
Champagne Bottle Lighter.........................$17.50 – 20.00
Football Lighter ....$12.50 – 15.00
Belt Buckle Lighter....................................$35.00 – 40.00

3rd Row:
Letter Opener and Case............................$12.50 – 15.00
Miniature Lighter ....$8.50 – 10.00
Miniature Harmonica on Chain ....$8.00 – 10.00
Hav-A-Shot, Bullet Carrier & Glasses........$15.00 – 20.00
Buddha Gods..$7.50 – 10.00 ea.
Spoon, Desco Stainless ....$1.50 – 2.50
Horse and Rider ....$15.00 – 20.00

Bottom Row:
Pliers in Original Box ....$25.00 – 30.00
Wrench in Original Box..............................$25.00 – 30.00

Page 48
Top row:
Negro Outhouse ....$30.00 – 40.00
Blue Pitchers ....$2.50 – 4.00 ea.
Clocks ....$6.00 – 7.50 ea.
Grandfather Clock......................................$9.00 – 11.00

2nd Row:
Blue Teakettle (Lid Lifts) ....$5.00 – 7.50
Souvenir Pitchers ....$3.00 – 4.00 ea.
Other Items..$2.00 – 4.00 ea.

3rd Row:
Shoes (Note the cat heads on two.)...............$5.00 – 6.50 ea.

4th Row:
1st, 4th, 5th, Shoes....................................$3.50 – 4.50 ea.
2nd Bisque Shoe ....$10.00 – 12.00
3rd Shoe, Outdoor Scene ....$10.00 – 12.00

5th Row:
Egg Cups...$12.00 – 15.00 ea.
Piano (2 Part)...$7.00 – 9.00
Dutch Clog Shoe Planter.............................$5.00 – 6.00
Bench ....$2.50 – 3.00

6th Row:
Stroller, Soldiers, Shoe ....$5.00 – 6.00 ea.
Covered Wagon ....$5.00 – 7.00
Heart box (32 Piece) ....$10.00 – 12.00
Cinderella Coach and Horses....................$12.50 – 15.00

Page 50
Top Row
Fans ....$8.00 – 10.00 ea.
Coolie Pincushion ....$17.50 – 20.00

2nd Row:
Whetstone ....$8.00 – 10.00
Boat..$12.00 – 15.00
Shamrocks...$1.00 – 1.50 ea.
Prayer Beads ....$25.00 – 30.00

Sewing Kit ....$15.00 – 20.00

Bottom Row:
Needle Packets ....$4.00 – 5.00 ea.

Page 52
Top Row:
Picnic Basket..$65.00 – 75.00

2nd Row:
Cigarette Dispenser.......................................$25.00 – 30.00
Trays ....$4.00 – 5.00 ea.

3rd Row:
Bamboo Dipper...$20.00 – 25.00
Salad Bowl..$6.00 – 7.50
Coaster Box and 6 Coasters ....$12.00 – 15.00

Page 54
Top Row:
Trays ....$4.00 – 5.50 ea.
Jack-O-Lantern ....$50.00 – 75.00

2nd Row:
Coaster ....$1.50 – 2.00
Purses ....$30.00 – 40.00 ea.

Page 56
Top Row:
Dog and Hat ....$5.00 – 7.50
Elephant and Lion ....$10.00 – 12.00 ea.
Dutch and Mexican Boy ....$8.00 – 10.00 ea.

2nd Row:
Sassy Girl (boy companion pictured page 111)...........$15.00 – 17.50
Black Girl..$35.00 – 50.00
Pig and Rabbit...$4.00 – 5.00 ea.
Dog and Cat ....$4.00 – 5.00 ea.

3rd Row:
Donkey Pulling Cart ....$8.00 – 10.00
Girl and Fat Boy..$12.50 – 15.00 ea.
Train..$7.00 – 8.00
Dog...$5.00 – 6.00

4th Row:
Sudanese Heads ....$30.00 – 35.00 ea.
Prim Lady and Tearful Girl............................$20.00 – 25.00 ea.
Man with Wheelbarrow ....$6.00 – 7.00
Duck Planter..$7.00 – 8.00

Page 58
Top Row:
Japanese Pair, Chalkware...............................$20.00 – 25.00 ea.
    Pair...$50.00 – 55.00
Oriental Bisque, Relief..................................$20.00 – 25.00 ea.
    Pair...$50.00 – 55.00

2nd Row:
Iris Wall Pocket...$17.50 – 20.00
Dutch Pair, Chalkware...................................$20.00 – 25.00 ea.
    Pair...$50.00 – 55.00

Cupped Saucer ....$5.00 – 7.50

Page 60
Top Row:
Rectangular Relief, Bisque (probably one of a pair) ...$35.00 – 40.00

2nd Row:
Round Relief Musical Couple, Bisque.......................$25.00 – 30.00 ea.
    Pair...$60.00 – 65.00
Swingers Relief...$20.00 – 25.00 ea.
    Pair...$50.00 – 55.00

3rd Row:
Heads, Crinoline Lined ....$20.00 – 22.50 ea.
    Pair...$45.00 – 50.00
Standing Colonials, Relief ....$17.50 – 20.00 ea.
    Pair...$40.00 – 45.00

4th Row:
Fall and Spring Plaques ....$6.00 – 8.00 ea.

Page 62
Top Row:
Fruit Shakers (3 Part)....................................$12.50 – 15.00
Fireside Shakers (5 Part, Includes Mustard) ....$25.00 – 30.00
Flowers (3 Part)...$20.00 – 25.00

2nd Row:
Cats and Birds...$12.00 – 15.00 pr.
Dutch Children..$12.00 – 15.00 pr.

3rd Row:
1st, 2nd Pair ....$8.50 – 10.00 pr.
Strawberry Set (3 Part)..................................$12.50 – 15.00
Toby Mug Type ....$20.00 – 25.00 pr.

4th Row:
Bears, Hugging ....$15.00 – 20.00
All other Pairs ....$10.00 – 12.50 pr.

5th Row:
All Pairs ....$9.00 – 10.00 pr.

Page 64
Top Row:
Creamer...$10.00 – 12.00
Toby Teapot...$50.00 – 60.00

2nd Row:
Floral Creamers...$12.50 – 15.00 ea.
Sugar, Creamer on Tray.................................$25.00 – 30.00

3rd Row:
Sugar and Creamer Sets ....$25.00 – 30.00

4th Row:
Teapots..$10.00 – 12.50 ea.
Sugar and Creamer Set...................................$17.50 – 20.00

Page 66
Top Row:
Tea Set with 4 Cups, Saucers, Plates ....$125.00 – 150.00

Tea Set with 6 Cups, Saucers, Plates ....$150.00 – 175.00
Gift Set in Case (Cobalt Blue Glass) ....$40.00 – 50.00

2nd Row:
Cottage Set (as shown)..$150.00 – 200.00

Page 68

Top Row:
Set of Six Mugs...$125.00 – 150.00

3rd Row:
Dog Tobies...$30.00 – 35.00 ea.
Lady ....$10.00 – 12.00
Skull ....$17.50 – 20.00
Devil..$35.00 – 40.00

4th Row:
1st Toby ....$20.00 – 25.00
2nd Toby ....$25.00 – 30.00
Indian ....$30.00 – 35.00

Page 70

Top Row:
Stein Imitation..$13.00 – 15.00
Bunny Handled Mug..$17.50 – 20.00
Endowed Lady Handled Mug ....$25.00 – 30.00

2nd Row:
1st, 3rd People Handled Mugs ....$15.00 – 20.00 ea.
Bickering Mug (Possibly of Set)..............................$20.00 – 25.00

3rd Row:
All Mugs ....$15.00 – 20.00 ea.

4th Row:
Nude Lady Handled Mug...$20.00 – 25.00
Parson Toby ....$75.00 – 100.00
Gentleman Toby ....$25.00 – 30.00

Page 72

Top Row:
Cowboy..$15.00 – 18.00 ea.
Dutch Girl ....$15.00 – 18.00
Japanese Girl ....$12.00 – 15.00
Vase (richly painted, gold trim) ....$12.50 – 15.00

2nd Row:
Vases..$3.00 – 5.00 ea.
Dog and Birds ....$4.00 – 5.00 ea.
Man ....$5.00 – 6.00

3rd Row:
Rabbits ....$5.00 – 6.50 ea.
Blue Vases ....$5.00 – 6.50 ea.
Scottie Dogs ....$7.50 – 10.00

4th Row:
Ox Cart..$4.50 – 6.00
Pig ....$8.00 – 10.00
Accordion Player ....$3.50 – 4.00
Spotted Dog ....$5.00 – 6.00
Scottie ....$6.00 – 7.50

5th Row:
Vases..$2.00 – 4.00 ea.
Animals ....$5.00 – 6.00 ea.

Page 74

Top Row:
Village (10 Pieces)..$30.00 – 35.00
Football Player ....$10.00 – 12.00

2nd Row:
Cars in Original Boxes..$75. 00 – 100.00 ea.
Wooden Puzzle ....$10.00 – 12.50
Rubber Knife...$7.50 – 10.00

3rd Row:
Football ....$17.50 – 20.00
Checkers..$12.50 – 15.00
Razzers..$5.00 – 6.00 ea.

Page 76

Top Row:
1st and 7th Vases ....$10.00 – 12.00 ea.
2nd, "Wedgwood" Vase..$4.00 – 5.00
3rd, 4th, and 5th Vases (3½ – 4") ....$6.00 – 7.50 ea.
6th Vase ....$12.50 – 15.00

2nd Row:
1st and 6th Vase ....$6.00 – 7.50 ea.
2nd, 3rd, 4th Vases...$15.00 – 17.50 ea.
5th Vase ....$25.00 – 30.00

3rd Row:
1st and 5th ....$25.00 – 30.00 pr.
2nd, 3rd, 4th Vases...$35.00 – 40.00 ea.

4th Row:
1st Vase ....$17.50 – 20.00
2nd Vase..$20.00 – 25.00
Dragon Vase ....$75.00 – 100.00

Page 78

Top Row:
Man, 15½"...$125.00 – 150.00
Lady, 14½"..$100.00 – 125.00

2nd Row:
Cupid and Swan ....$30.00 – 35.00
Cupid Artist...$65.00 – 75.00
Cupid Standing ....$35.00 – 40.00

3rd Row:
"Hummel-like" Boy and Girl....................................$25.00 – 35.00 ea.
Cupid and Heart ....$65.00 – 75.00
Seated Musician ....$30.00 – 35.00

Page 80

Top Row:
Bust of Man...$25.00 – 30.00
Lady Vase ....$22.50 – 25.00

2nd Row:
Caped Boy and Girl ....$25.00 – 30.00 ea.

Mexican with Donkey (Approx. 8") ....$25.00 – 30.00
Lady with Basket ....$17.50 – 20.00

3rd Row:
Colonial Man ....$12.00 – 15.00
Japanese Samurai ....$17.50 – 20.00
Peasant Girl Planter...$45.00 – 55.00

Page 82
Top Row:
1st, 2nd, 4th, and 5th Children ....$7.50 – 10.00 ea.
3rd Boy and Boy with Pig..$10.00 – 12.50 ea.

2nd Row:
Girl on Fence...$12.50 – 15.00
Girl in Cape..$12.50 – 15.00
Girl with Geese ....$25.00 – 30.00
Girls with Baskets ....$20.00 – 25.00 ea.

3rd Row:
Musicians ....$10.00 – 12.50 ea.

4th Row:
Girl with Doll ....$10.00 – 12.50
Girl with Accordion ....$8.50 – 10.00
Baby with Bee ....$20.00 – 25.00
Double Figure with Umbrella ....$10.00 – 12.50
Tiny Girl in Green...$4.50 – 5.00

Page 84
Top Row:
Boy and Girl (approx. 8") ....$35.00 – 40.00 ea.
  Pair ....$80.00 – 90.00

2nd Row:
Girl and Doll ....$40.00 – 50.00
Children with Boat..$35.00 – 45.00
Children with Umbrella ....$35.00 – 45.00

3rd Row:
Walking Boy (Larger of Two) ....$20.00 – 25.00
Artist and Palette ....$40.00 – 45.00
Umbrella Boy ....$20.00 – 25.00
Walking Boy (Smaller of Two) ....$12.50 – 15.00
Hiker ....$12.50 – 15.00

4th Row:
Girls with Geese..$25.00 – 30.00
Girl Feeding Geese ....$15.00 – 17.50
Girls with Baskets ....$20.00 – 25.00 ea.

Page 86
Top Row:
Lady and Gentleman, Paired......................................$30.00 – 35.00 ea.

2nd Row:
Dutch Children..$17.50 – 20.00 ea.
Lady Holding Hat ....$20.00 – 25.00
Dancing Lady..$20.00 – 25.00

3rd Row:
Tambourine Player...$20.00 – 25.00

Dancer..$25.00 – 30.00
Tiered Skirted Lady ....$25.00 – 30.00

Page 88
Top Row:
Green Pixies ....$15.00 – 17.50 ea.
Planter Pixie ....$15.00 – 17.50

2nd Row:
Elves Riding Insects/Animals....................................$25.00 – 30.00 ea.
3rd Row:
Mushroom Elves ....$10.00 – 15.00 ea.
Elf Astride Insect ....$25.00 – 30.00

4th Row:
Pink Suited Elves ....$15.00 – 20.00 ea.

Page 90
Top Row:
First and Third Couple ....$25.00 – 30.00 ea.
Coach ....$75.00 – 80.00

2nd Row:
Couple with Bench, Artist Signed ....$40.00 – 50.00
Standing Couple...$30.00 – 35.00
Seated Couple ....$17.50 – 20.00
Seated Couple, Small, Artist Signed.............................$30.00 – 35.00

3rd Row:
1st and 3rd Courting Couple ....$22.50 – 25.00 ea.
Seated Red Haired Couple ....$12.50 – 15.00

Bottom Row:
Oriental Couple...$20.00 – 25.00
Dutch Children Toothbrush Holder ....$25.00 – 30.00

Page 92
Top Row:
Girl, 12" tall ....$30.00 – 40.00
2nd and 5th Dancers...$20.00 – 25.00 ea.
3rd and 4th Dancers ....$17.50 – 20.00 ea.

2nd Row:
1st and 6th Small Figures.......................................$8.50 – 10.00 ea.
2nd and 5th Men, nice detail....................................$20.00 – 25.00 ea.
3rd Girl with Fan...$10.00 – 12.50
4th Male Musician ....$12.00 – 15.00

3rd Row:
1st and 5th Small Figures.......................................$6.00 – 7.00 ea.
2nd Performer, Mate to Above ....$8.50 – 10.00
Reclining Man...$12.50 – 15.00
Couple ....$8.50 – 10.00

Page 94
Top Row:
Oriental Pair ....$50.00 – 65.00
Trousered Oriental Pair ....$50.00 – 65.00

2nd Row:
First Pair Oriental Pair ....$40.00 – 50.00
Black Based Orientals...$35.00 – 45.00

3rd Row:
Coolie Hatted Pair...$25.00 – 27.50
Animated Pair Orientals....................................$30.00 – 35.00

4th Row:
Flared Trousered Pair...$35.00 – 40.00
Second Pair...$35.00 – 40.00

Page 97
Top Row:
Colonial Couple ....$125.00 – 150.00 pr.

2nd Row:
Couple in Blue and Pink, 12"..................$95.00 – 100.00

3rd Row:
Hatted Pair, Approx. 12".........................$100.00 – 120.00
Courting Couple, Approx. 12"....................$65.00 – 75.00

Bottom Row:
Musicians Couple, Approx. 10"..................$65.00 – 75.00
Seated pair, 6".....................................$35.00 – 40.00

Page 98
Top Row:
Hatted Colonials, Approx.12"pr ....$65.00 – 75.00
Red-Haired Colonials, 11½" pr...................$35.00 – 40.00

2nd Row:
First and Third Pair, Approx. 10" ....$50.00 – 60.00
Second Pair Colonials, 11½"pr ....$40.00 – 45.00

3rd Row:
First and Fourth Pairs, Approx. 6" pr..........$17.50 – 20.00
Musical Pair ....$40.00 – 45.00
Pair in Blue Tones.................................$17.50 – 20.00

Page 99
Top Row:
Musical Couples....................................$25.00 – 30.00

2nd Row:
First Pair (Bisque), Approx. 10" ....$75.00 – 85.00
Second Pair ....$20.00 – 25.00
Pair Dancers (Bisque), 10".......................$35.00 – 40.00

3rd Row:
1st and 3rd Pair, Seated..........................$50.00 – 60.00
2nd Pair, Orientals Bisque, Approx. 9" ....$50.00 – 60.00

Page 100
Top Row:
Incense Burners.............................$15.00 – 20.00 ea.

2nd Row:
Orientals (end of row)....................$20.00 – 22.50 ea.
Mandolin and Flute Players ....$15.00 – 17.50 ea.
3rd and 4th Figures ....$15.00 – 20.00 ea.

3rd Row:
1st Pair ....$30.00 – 35.00 ea.

3rd Double Figure, Boy & Girl...................$10.00 – 12.00
Girl in Lavender (probably one of pair)........$15.00 – 17.50
Colonial Man (probably one of pair) ....$15.00 – 17.50

4th Row:
Reclining Oriental................................$10.00 – 12.00
Smaller Boy Blue...................................$9.00 – 10.00
Larger Boy Blue..................................$13.50 – 15.00
Seated Tyrolienne Boy............................$12.00 – 15.00

Page 103
Top Row:
1st and 5th Orientals ....$17.50 – 20.00 ea.
2nd and 4th Orientals ....$25.00 – 30.00 ea.
3rd (seen as lamp base).........................$25.00 – 30.00

2nd Row:
1st Colonial ....$20.00 – 25.00
Lady with Dog ....$20.00 – 25.00
Lady with Net Dress ....$50.00 – 60.00
Gaucho with Guitar ....$15.00 – 17.50
Lady in Pink and White ....$10.00 – 12.00

3rd Row:
Colonial in Tri-Cornered Hat,10" ....$20.00 – 25.00
Lady with Horn, Approx. 10" ....$20.00 – 25.00
Lady with Accordion, Approx. 10" ....$20.00 – 25.00

Page 104
Top Row:
1st, 2nd, 4th Lady............................$5.00 – 6.00 ea.
Dutch Girl with Buckets ....$17.50 – 20.00

2nd Row:
1st and 4th Colonials.......................$12.50 – 15.00 ea.
2nd and 3rd ....$13.00 – 17.50 ea.
5th Lady ....$8.00 – 10.00

3rd Row:
1st and 5th Musicians.......................$12.50 – 15.00 ea.
2nd and 4th Ladies ....$15.00 – 17.00 ea.
Lady with Flower Basket ....$18.00 – 20.00

4th Row:
1st, 2nd, 3rd, Colonials ....$12.50 – 15.00 ea.
4th Lady ....$20.00 – 25.00
Lady with Dog ....$30.00 – 40.00

Page 105
Top Row:
Bride and Groom, 4¼"..............................$25.00 – 30.00
Bride and Groom, 5"..............................$40.00 – 45.00
Bride and Groom, 3½"..............................$20.00 – 22.50

2nd Row:
Wood-Like Dwarves, 1st and 6th ....$8.00 – 10.00 ea.
Wood-Like Dwarves, 2nd thru 5th ....$10.00 – 12.00 ea.

3rd Row:
1st and 2nd Ladies ....$3.00 – 5.00 ea.
Negro Match Holder ....$20.00 – 25.00
Shoe Shine Boy...................................$40.00 – 50.00

African Boy...$20.00 – 25.00
Uncle Sam, 5"...$20.00 – 25.00

4th Row:
Indian Salt Shakers (each end)....................................$12.00 – 15.00 pr.
3rd and 6th Indian ....$8.00 – 10.00 ea.
4th Chief..$25.00 – 30.00
5th Chief..$30.00 – 35.00

5th Row:
Ballerina with Net Skirt ....$15.00 – 20.00
2nd, 3rd, 6th Ladies ....$10.00 – 12.50 ea.
4th Lady in Yellow Skirt, Bisque ....$25.00 – 30.00
5th Dancer..$8.00 – 10.00

Page 106
Lamp ....$125.00 – 150.00
Stork...$75.00 – 100.00

Page 109
Bisque Colonial Pair, 15½"......................................$200.00 – 225.00
Bisque Cavalier, 14" ....$75.00 – 100.00

Page 110
Top Row:
Satsuma-like Teapot (other pieces likely)..................$40.00 – 50.00
"Hummel-like" Soldier Children ....$40.00 – 50.00
"Hummel-like" Children with Boat...........................$40.00 – 45.00

2nd Row:
Children Planters...$35.00 – 45.00 pr.
Negro Shelf Sitter ....$20.00 – 25.00
Horned Bugle Boy Devil in Bisque ....$20.00 – 25.00
Cupid and Shell Planters...$50.00 – 55.00 pr.

3rd Row:
Celluloid Cowboy with Wind-Up Bucking Horse.....$75.00 – 100.00
"Hummel-like" Children with Dogs ....$40.00 – 45.00 ea.

Page 111
Top Row:
Cow Creamer ....$30.00 – 35.00

2nd Row:
Bird Shaker and Mustard Set ....$22.50 – 25.00

Old Oriental ....$12.50 – 15.00
Sassy Boy Planter (mate shown on page 57).............$15.00 – 17.50

3rd Row:
Strawberry Shakers in Basket ....$12.00 – 15.00
Pink Cigarette Box (Trays Within)............................$20.00 – 25.00
Black and White Cup and Saucer ....$10.00 – 12.50
Deer...$4.00 – 6.00

4th Row:
Demitasse Cup and Saucer..$10.00 – 20.00 ea.
Ash Tray to Cigarette Box (Alone).............................$3.00 – 3.50 ea.
Coffee Pot Shakers pr ....$10.00 – 20.00 pr.
Pixie Toothpick Holder...$10.00 – 12.00

5th Row:
Odd Tea Kettle Shakers ....$4.00 – 5.00 ea.

Page 112
Top Row:
Match Safe Wall Hanger...$35.00 – 40.00
Grampa with Bug ....$10.00 – 12.00
Dutch Girl Marmalade ....$20.00 – 25.00

2nd Row:
Lighted (Electric) Wall Plaque, Bisque ....$40.00 – 50.00
Large Duck Plaque...$15.00 – 20.00
Mexican Toothpick Holder..$6.00 – 7.00

3rd Row:
Fruit Plate for Hanging (shown upside down)..............$8.00 – 10.00
Smaller Duck Plaque..$10.00 – 12.50
Cup and Saucer ....$12.50 – 15.00

4th Row:
Donkey Cart Planter...$3.50 – 4.50
Decorative Tray ....$2.50 – 3.50
Strawberry Covered Jar...$12.00 – 15.00
Cobalt Blue Powder Jar, Hinged................................$65.00 – 75.00

5th Row:
Dog Relish (head lifts for serving capacity) ....$35.00 – 45.00
Cow Creamer ....$30.00 – 35.00

Price Guide for Occupied Japan
Third Series

Page 8
Top Row:
1st and 3rd Flower Cupids, 4" ....$25.00 – 30.00 ea.
2nd Cupid w/Flower Snail, 4½" x 6" ....$30.00 – 35.00

2nd Row:
1st and 6th Cupid on Sled, 5" ....$30.00 – 35.00 ea.
2nd, 3rd, 4th, and 5th Musicians, 3¼" ....$7.50 – 9.00 ea.

3rd Row:
1st Butterfly Babe, 3¼" ....$20.00 – 22.50
2nd, 3rd, 4th, and 5th Angels, 2" to 2½" ....$5.00 – 6.00 ea.
6th, 7th, 8th, and 9th Musician, 2½" ....$5.00 – 6.00 ea.

4th Row:
1st and 6th Angel Vases, 7½" ....$50.00 – 55.00 ea.
2nd Candleholder, 6" ....$40.00 – 45.00
3rd Angel Drummer, 5¼" ....$25.00 – 30.00
4th Angel w/Horn, 5" ....$22.50 – 25.00
5th Arrow Repair Cupid, 7" ....$40.00 – 45.00

5th Row:
1st Cupid w/Donkey, 4" ....$22.50 – 25.00
2nd Nude on Seahorse, 3½" ....$17.50 – 20.00
3rd Angel Planter, 3½" ....$15.00 – 17.50
4th and 5th Cupid w/Moon, 3½" ....$8.00 – 10.00 ea.
6th and 7th Angel Bud Vase, 2¾" ....$10.00 – 12.50 ea.

Page 10
Top Row:
Cow, 2¾" x 4" ....$8.00 – 10.00
Elsie, 3½" ....$17.50 – 20.00
Squirrels, 4½" x 5" ....$17.50 – 20.00
Pig, 2½" x 3½" ....$10.00 – 12.50
Cow set, large 2¾" x 4" ....$20.00 – 22.50
Cow set, small 1¼" ....$20.00 – 22.50

2nd Row:
Horse, 2¼" ....$4.00 – 5.00
Cat, 2" ....$4.00 – 5.00
Cats, 1¼" ....$6.00 – 7.50
Dogs, 2¼" ....$8.00 – 10.00
Dogs, terriers, 3½" ....$15.00 – 17.50
Scotties, three white or black ....$6.00 – 8.00
Dogs in Basket, 3¼" ....$12.50 – 15.00
Dog, blue, 1¾" x 3¼" ....$6.00 – 7.50
Dog, 3¾" ....$12.50 – 15.00

3rd Row:
Dog w/Lamp, 2" ....$3.00 – 4.00
Dog, begging, 2½" ....$4.00 – 5.00
Dog w/Pups, 2⅛" ....$7.00 – 7.50
Poodle, 3" ....$10.00 – 12.50
Shepherd, 1¾" x 3¼" ....$5.00 – 6.00
Dog, green, 2" x 3" ....$5.00 – 6.00
Dog, pair, 2" ....$7.50 – 10.00
Dog w/Horn, 3½" ....$7.00 – 8.50
Puppies, 2" ....$4.00 – 5.00

4th Row:
Dog, 4½" x 5½" ....$15.00 – 17.50
Dog, 5½" x 7" ....$15.00 – 17.50
Terrier pair, 4½" x 7" ....$25.00 – 27.50
Terrier, 4" ....$15.00 – 17.50
Puppies in Basket, 2½" ....$12.50 – 15.00

5th Row:
Lady bugs (3), 2¼" x 2½" ....$6.00 – 7.50 ea.
Monkeys, white (3), 1¾" ....$4.00 – 5.00 ea.
Monkeys (3), 2¼" ....$6.00 – 7.50 ea.
Monkeys, "Speak, see, and hear no evil" ....$10.00 – 12.50
Cat w/Fiddle, 2" ....$6.00 – 7.50
Rabbit, 1" x 2¼" ....$6.00 – 7.50

Page 12
Top Row:
Ducks, 5" to 6½" wall plaques ....$22.50 – 25.00 ea.

2nd Row:
Chicken pr., 5" ....$17.50 – 20.00
Bird, 3" ....$3.00 – 4.50
Ducks, 4" ....$10.00 – 12.50

3rd Row:
Jay, 2½" ....$4.00 – 5.00
Crane, 3¼" ....$6.00 – 8.00
Peacock, 3⅛" ....$6.00 – 8.00
Bird, 2¼" ....$3.00 – 4.00
Bird, 2½" ....$4.00 – 5.00

4th Row:
Peacock, 7" ....$25.00 – 27.50
Chicken on Nest, 5⅞", 2 piece ....$30.00 – 35.00
Flamingo, 5½" ....$12.50 – 15.00
Flamingo, 7¼" ....$25.00 – 27.50

5th Row:
Gazelles, 3¾" ....$7.00 – 8.50
Frog w/Mandolin, 3½" ....$15.00 – 17.50
Frog w/Violin, 4¼" ....$17.50 – 20.00
Frog w/Accordion, 4" ....$15.00 – 17.50
Penguin Bookends, pr., 4" ....$20.00 – 25.00

Page 14
Top Row:
Red bowl, 4¾" ....$6.00 – 7.50
Horse Pulling Wagon Ash Tray ....$6.00 – 7.50
Tray, 8¾" ....$8.00 – 10.00
Horse pulling wagon, 3¼", diamond, Ash Tray ....$6.00 – 7.50
Wash Line Ash Tray ....$6.00 – 7.50
Tray, 9¼" ....$8.00 – 10.00
Lady Ash Tray ....$12.50 – 15.00
Ceramic Cigarette Lighter, 2⅞" ....$15.00 – 20.00
North Carolina Ash Tray ....$12.50 – 15.00

2nd Row:
"Wedgewood"- type 2⅝" Ash Tray ....$8.00 – 10.00

"Wedgewood"- type, Niagara Falls Rainbow Bridge ....$18.00 – 20.00
Metal Lighter on Tray, 5¼" ....$12.50 – 15.00
Donkey Pulling Ashes..$6.00 – 7.50
Cigarette Potties ....$12.50 – 15.00
Dog Hydrant, 2 x 2¼", No Parking..................................$4.00 – 5.00
Cigarette Urn, 3" ....$4.00 – 5.00
Lady Spade Ash Tray..$6.00 – 7.50
Metal Four-Piece Set, 5¾"..$22.50 – 25.00

3rd Row:
Indian Metal Cigarette Lighter....................................$20.00 – 22.50
Urn-type Lighters, 2¾" and 3¼"..................................$8.00 – 10.00 ea.
Round Lighter, ball top, 4¼" ....$15.00 – 17.50
Giant Lighter, 3" x 4"...$15.00 – 17.50
Lighter Set, 3¼" x 6¼" ....$22.50 – 25.00
"Crown" Lighter, 2½"..$10.00 – 12.50
Gun Lighter, 2" ....$12.50 – 15.00
Gun Lighter, 2½" ....$12.50 – 15.00
Camera Lighter ....$30.00 – 35.00

4th Row:
Hand Warmer, 3¾" x 2½"...$25.00 – 30.00
Horse Shoe Ash Tray w/Horse, 4⅝"............................$20.00 – 25.00
Ash Tray, 3½"..$2.50 – 3.00
Binoculars, 7 x 50, Field 710.......................................$50.00 – 65.00
Opera Glasses..$25.00 – 30.00
Ash Tray, 3⅝"..$3.00 – 3.50
Binoculars w/Case, 8 x 30, Field 850 ....$65.00 – 75.00
Horse Ash Tray, 4⅞" ....$6.00 – 7.50

5th Row:
Cigarette Box w/four 3" trays, 3¾" x 2¾".................$20.00 – 22.50
Cigarette Box w/two 2½" x 3½" trays, 3½" x 4½".....$18.00 – 20.00
Colonial ladies Cigarette Box with 2¾" x 3¾"tray......$20.00 – 25.00
Violets Cigarette Box w/two 2¾" x 3¾" trays............$22.50 – 25.00
Indian Ash Tray, 2¼" x 3¼" ....$6.00 – 7.50
Ash Tray, 2¾" sq. ....$3.00 – 3.50

Page 16
Left Column Top:
Ash Tray, 3" ....$4.00 – 5.00
Chicken Clicker, 1½"...$5.00 – 6.00
Elephant on World Pencil Trimmer............................$15.00 – 17.50
Ash Tray, 3¼"..$4.00 – 5.00
Leaf, 5½"...$4.00 – 5.00
Painted Tray, 4"...$4.00 – 5.00
Ash Tray, 5¼", Statue of Liberty................................$12.50 – 15.00
Nut Bowl, 2¾" ....$4.00 – 5.00
Tray, 4¾" ....$3.50 – 5.00

Center Column Top:
Ash Tray, 4¾", Indianapolis, Ind...................................$4.00 – 5.00
Bowl, 5" Swan mark on back..$6.00 – 7.50
Leaf, 6"...$6.00 – 7.50
Leaf, 5", "Economy" ....$4.00 – 5.00
Ash Tray, 4¾", palm trees..$4.00 – 5.00

Right Column Top:
Ash Tray, 5½"...$5.00 – 6.00
Divided Trays, 5¼" each representing the following:
    Florida...$6.00 – 7.50
    U. S. Capitol..$6.00 – 7.50

Statue of Liberty ....$12.50 – 15.00
Niagara Falls ....$6.00 – 7.50
Atlantic City...$6.00 – 7.50
Coney Island ....$12.50 – 15.00

Page 18
Top:
Planter Couple w/Rabbits, 5¼" x 7¼" ....$150.00 – 200.00

Right:
Cupid w/Gold Rings and Lady w/Lyre, 8¼" x 9¼".$225.00 – 250.00

Bottom:
Courting Couple w/Lambs, 8¼" x 9¼"....................$300.00 – 350.00

Page 20
Top Row:
Orientals, 6" ....$20.00 ea. or 45.00 – 50.00 pr.
Seated colonials, 7" ....$72.50 ea. or $145.00 – 160.00 pr.
Country Couple, 6¼" male and 6" female..$20.00 ea. or 40.00 – 45.00 pr.

2nd Row:
1st and 6th pr. Vase, 5" ....$22.50 ea. or 50.00 – 55.00 pr.
Couple, 9¼" ....$45.00 ea. or 90.00 – 100.00 pr.
Fence-Leaning Couple, 9" ....$57.50 ea. or 115.00 – 120.00 pr.

3rd Row:
Flower Gathers, 10¼" ....$65.00 ea. or 130.00 – 140.00 pr.
Plumbed Hat Couple, 9¾" ....$60.00 ea. or 120.00 – 130.00 pr.
Pastoral Couple, 10¼"..........................$65.00 ea. or 130.00 – 140.00 pr.

Page 22
Top Row:
Colonial Man, 7"...$25.00 – 27.50
Colonial Man, 7"...$17.50 – 30.00
Lady w/Basket, 7"...$35.00 – 37.50
Lady w/Dog, 6"...$22.50 – 25.00
Man, 6½"...$15.00 – 17.50
Windy Lady, 6½"..$25.00 – 27.50

2nd Row:
Couple, 3½"..$15.00 – 17.50
Lady w/Basket, 6"...$22.50 – 25.00
Lady Shell Planter, 5½" x 6½" ....$50.00 – 55.00
Dance, 5"...$15.00 – 17.50

3rd Row:
Lady, 4¾"...$15.00 – 17.50
Lady, 4"..$12.50 – 15.00
Horn Player, 4½" ....$15.00 – 17.50
Colonial Man, 5"..$12.50 – 15.00
Lady w/Goose, 5⅝"..$50.00 – 55.00

4th Row:
Lady w/Fan, 10½"..$65.00 – 75.00
Lady, 10¼"...$60.00 – 65.00
Man w/Flowers, 10¼"...$60.00 – 65.00
Man w/Violin, 9" ....$55.00 – 60.00

Page 24
Top Row:
Pink Crocheted Dress, 6" ....$40.00 – 45.00

Nude, 4¾" ....$12.50 – 15.00
Pink Baby, 5½" ....$22.50 – 25.00

2nd Row:
Feather or Go Go Dancer, 13" ....$40.00 – 45.00

3rd Row:
Yellow and White Crocheted Dress, 8" ....$40.00 – 45.00
Kewpie, 2¾" ....$17.50 – 20.00
Feather Dancer, 4¼" ....$12.50 – 15.00
Blue Crochet Boy, 7" ....$40.00 – 45.00

Page 26

Top Row:
Water Lily in Box ....$7.50 – 10.00 ea.

2nd Row:
Dolls in Basket, 4⅝" x 3" ....$60.00 – 65.00
Quints in Box, 2¾" ....$85.00 – 95.00

3rd Row:
Dog, Squeaker...$8.00 – 10.00
Doll, China, 3¼" ....$25.00 – 30.00
Doll, China, 3" ....$17.50 – 20.00
Doll, Black, 3¼" ....$40.00 – 45.00
Doll, 7"...$50.00 – 55.00

4th Row:
Ducks, 4" w/Hangers and Spring Legs ....$6.00 – 7.50
Magnifying Glass......................................$10.00 – 12.50

5th Row:
Shell w/Paper Flowers, 1¼"........................$2.50 – 3.00

6th Row:
Water Lily ....$7.50 – 10.00
Celluloid Dog House................................$10.00 – 12.50
Celluloid "Happy House" Pencil Holder ......$20.00 – 25.00
Paper Monkey Squeeze Accordion, 1½" x 2½".......$3.00 – 3.50
Celluloid Duck, 4½" ....$17.50 – 20.00

Page 28

"Blue Willow" or "Disney"
Two Place Setting (9 pieces)......................$95.00 – 100.00
Four Place Setting (13 pieces) ....$130.00 – 145.00
Six Place Setting (23 pieces).....................$250.00 – 275.00
Six Place Setting w/Serving Pieces (26 pieces).......$300.00 – 325.00

Florals or Other Decorating
Two Place...$30.00 – 35.00
Three Place...$40.00 – 45.00
Four Place..$50.00 – 55.00
Four Place w/Serving.................................$70.00 – 85.00
Five Place...$85.00 – 90.00
Six Place..$95.00 – 100.00
Six Place w/Serving ....$115.00 – 125.00

Top Row (Blue Willow):
Creamer, 1½" to 2" ....$12.50 – 15.00
Cup and saucer, 2¾" to 3½" ....$15.00 – 17.50
Plate, 3¾" to 4½" ....$12.00 – 15.00
Sugar w/Lid, 2" to 2¼" ....$17.50 – 20.00

Teapot w/Lid, 3¼" to 3¾" ....$40.00 – 45.00

2nd Row:
Lustre ware: 4 piece set............................$65.00 – 75.00
Luster Creamer, 1½".................................$6.00 – 7.50
Platter, Blue Willow 6" ....$35.00 – 40.00
Tomato Teapot, 2" x 4"..............................$15.00 – 20.00
Tomato Cup and Saucer............................$7.50 – 10.00
Tomato Sugar w/Lid, 1½" x 2"....................$10.00 – 12.00
Tomato Creamer (not shown).....................$7.50 – 10.00

3rd Row:
Chest, 1½" high.......................................$6.00 – 7.50
Set: "Pico" w/2¾"tray, teapot, creamer and sugar, 2 cups
    and saucers..$22.50 – 25.00
Bench, 1¾"..$4.00 – 5.00
Refrigerator, 3½"......................................$18.00 – 20.00
Set: 2¼" tray, w/cr/sug.............................$10.00 – 12.50
Sink, 2" x 3"..$18.00 – 20.00
Set: tray, teapot, pitcher, cups and saucers, cr/sug.......$20.00 – 22.50
Set: teapot, cr/sug, 4 cups and saucers.........................$22.50 – 25.00
Refrigerator, Philco, 2½"...........................$12.50 – 15.00
Cabinet, 2¼"...$10.00 – 12.50
Dry sink, 2"..$10.00 – 12.50
Sets: as shown marked HKATO.................$15.00 – 17.50

4th Row:
Chair, 3"..$8.00 – 10.00
Chest, 1¾"..$7.50 – 9.00
Couch, 3"...$12.50 – 15.00
Chair, 3"..$10.00 – 12.50
Dresser, 2⅛"..$6.00 – 7.00
Chair, 1⅞"...$5.00 – 6.00
Piano, 1¾"...$6.00 – 7.50
Set: 1½" chest, 2¼" bed, 1¾" lamp ....$15.00 – 17.50

5th Row:
Elephant w/Flag Cup, 1¾"..........................$8.00 – 10.00
Same, Sugar w/Lid, 2½"............................$10.00 – 12.50
Same, Creamer, 1½"..................................$8.00 – 10.00
Set: 1½" teapot, creamer, sug w/lid (not shown).........$18.00 – 20.00
Set: teapot, creamer, 2 cups and saucers, sugar with lid
    (not shown) ....$22.50 – 25.00

6th Row:
Set: sugar w/lid, creamer (not shown), 4 cups and
    saucers..$45.00 – 50.00
Set: sugar w/lid, creamer, 4 cups and saucers.............$55.00 – 65.00

Page 30

Top Row:
Boy w/Broken Sprinkler, 4½".......................$30.00 – 35.00
Basket Girl, 5½".......................................$27.50 – 30.00
Basket Boy, 5¾".......................................$27.50 – 30.00
Flute-Playing Boy, 4½" ....$20.00 – 22.50

2nd Row:
Skier, 4½"..$25.00 – 27.50
Boy w/Begging Dog, 5"..............................$35.00 – 40.00
Hiker, 4"..$15.00 – 17.50
Girl w/Basket, 4½"....................................$15.00 – 17.50
Boy w/Duck, 3¾".......................................$27.50 – 30.00

3rd Row:

1st and 3rd pr, 5½" (probably bookends)..$35.00 ea. or 75.00 – 80.00 pr.
Umbrella, pair, 6"...$35.00 – 40.00

4th Row:

1st and 3rd Tyrolean pair, 5" ....$40.00 – 45.00 ea.
Gardening pair, 5½"...$50.00 – 60.00

Page 32

Top Row:

Boy w/Parrot, 5" ....$10.00 – 12.50
Boy w/Guitar, 4" ....$7.50 – 9.00
Boy w/Dog, 4¾" ....$10.00 – 12.50
Girl, 4"...$8.00 – 10.00
Boy w/Horn, 3½"..$6.00 – 8.00
Boy w/Chick, 2½"..$4.00 – 5.00
Girl on Fence, 4"..$8.00 – 10.00
Boxing Boy, 4½"...$12.50 – 15.00

2nd Row:

Boy w/Cello, 5"...$10.00 – 12.50
According Girl, 4½"..$8.00 – 10.00
Horn Player, 4"..$10.00 – 12.50
Sax Player, 4½"...$8.00 – 10.00
Girl w/Dog, 4¼"...$8.00 – 10.00
Guitar Player, 4½" ....$12.50 – 15.00
Book Carrier, 4"...$8.00 – 10.00

3rd Row:

Boy w/Hat, 5" ....$8.00 – 10.00
Newsboy, 5½"..$10.00 – 12.50
Walker, 6"...$18.00 – 20.00
Horn Player, 9½"...$27.50 – 30.00
Tuba Player, 5"..$10.00 – 12.50
Musketeer, 5"...$8.00 – 10.00
Hiker, 4"...$10.00 – 12.50

4th Row:

Accordian Player, 4" ....$8.00 – 10.00
2nd to 6th Musicians, 2⅝"..$6.00 – 7.50 ea.
Boy w/Dog, 4⅛"...$12.50 – 15.00
Violin Player, 3¾" ....$10.00 – 12.50
Flutist, 4½"..$8.00 – 10.00

Page 34

Top Row:

1st set "Merit"..$10.00 – 12.50
2nd set "Ucagco"...$10.00 – 12.50
3rd set "Trimont China"..$10.00 – 12.50
4th set "MIOJ"...$10.00 – 12.50

2nd Row:

1st, 2nd, 3rd sets "Nasco Fine China" ....$8.00 – 10.00
4th set "MIOJ"...$10.00 – 12.50

3rd Row:

1st and 5th sets "Shofu China" ....$12.50 – 15.00
2nd and 3rd sets "Ucagco"..$12.50 – 15.00
4th set "Merit"..$10.00 – 12.50

4th Row:

1st set "Merit"...$12.50 – 15.00

2nd set "Gold China"...$12.50 – 15.00
3rd set "Merit"..$10.00 – 12.50
4th set "Noritake" ....$10.00 – 12.50
5th set "Jyoto China"..$10.00 – 12.50

5th Row:

1st set "Jyoto China"...$10.00 – 12.50
2nd set "Crown w/B inside" in red ....$12.50 – 15.00
3rd set "Spring Violets"...$12.50 – 15.00
4th set "Elephant Head"..$12.50 – 15.00
5th set "Elephant Head"..$17.50 – 20.00

6th Row:

1st set gold horse w/gray knight ....$17.50 – 20.00
2nd set "Shofu China" ....$15.00 – 17.50
3rd set "Wako China" ....$17.50 – 20.00
4th set "Chugai China" ....$15.00 – 17.50

Page 36

Top Row:

Semi-nudes plate ....$10.00 – 12.50
"Leawile China" (cup only)...$15.00 – 17.50
2nd set "Ironstone Ware"...$15.00 – 17.50
3rd set "Trimont China"..$12.50 – 15.00
4th set "Maruta China" ....$17.50 – 20.00

2nd Row:

1st set "Ucagco China" ....$10.00 – 12.50
2nd set "Trimont China"..$10.00 – 12.50
3rd set "MK" in wreath...$10.00 – 12.50
4th set "MIOJ"...$8.00 – 10.00

3rd Row:

1st set "Merit"...$8.00 – 10.00
2nd set "MIOJ"...$8.00 – 10.00
3rd set "Aiyo China"...$12.50 – 15.00
4th set "Gold China"...$10.00 – 12.50

4th Row:

1st set "Merit" (leaf shaped) ....$18.00 – 20.00
2nd set "Shofu China" ....$15.00 – 17.50
3rd set "Saji Fancy China"...$15.00 – 17.50
4th set"MIOJ"...$8.00 – 10.00
5th and 6th "MIOJ"...$18.00 – 20.00 ea.

5th Row:

1st and 2nd sets "Saji Fancy China" ....$20.00 – 22.50
3rd set "Ohashi China" ....$17.50 – 20.00
4th set "MIOJ" (thatch house river scene)...........................$15.00 – 17.50
5th set "MIOJ" (red pagoda scene)....................................$10.00 – 12.50

6th Row:

1st set "Trimont China" ....$15.00 – 17.50
2nd set "MIOJ"...$15.00 – 17.50
3rd set "Ucagco China" "Ivory" pattern ....$12.50 – 15.00
4th set "Saji Fancy China" ....$10.00 – 12.50

Page 38

Top Row:

1st set "Merit"...$10.00 – 12.50
2nd set "MIOJ"...$10.00 – 12.50
3rd and 4th sets "Ucago" ....$10.00 – 12.50

Blue flowered cup "Trimont China"................................$6.00 – 7.50
5th set "Gold Castle" ....$10.00 – 12.50

2nd Row:
1st set "MIOJ"...$18.00 – 20.00
2nd set "MIOJ"..$18.00 – 20.00
Orange dragon cup...$12.50 – 15.00
3rd set "Lucky China" ....$15.00 – 17.50
4th set "MIOJ"..$18.00 – 20.00
5th set "Sak China"...$15.00 – 17.50
6th set "Gold China"...$10.00 – 12.50

3rd Row:
1st set "MIOJ"...$8.00 – 10.00
2nd set "Merit"...$8.00 – 10.00
3rd set "Saji Fancy China" ....$12.50 – 15.00
4th set "KS" ....$6.00 – 8.00
5th set "High Mount" ....$6.00 – 8.00
6th set "Ardalt" No. 6075 ....$10.00 – 12.50

4th Row:
1st set "Ardalt" No. 6143.....................................$17.50 – 20.00
2nd set "Merit"...$12.50 – 15.00
3rd set "Sango China"...$12.50 – 15.00
4th set "Ucagco" ....$12.50 – 15.00
5th set "Celebrate" ....$12.50 – 15.00

5th Row:
1st set "MIOJ" (Designed by Aurger of Miami) ....$17.50 – 20.00
2nd set "Beteson China," J. B....................................$10.00 – 12.50
3rd set "Celebrate" ....$10.00 – 12.50
4th set "MIOJ" ....$6.00 – 8.00
5th set "MIOJ" ....$8.00 – 10.00
6th set "MIOJ" ....$6.00 – 8.00

6th Row:
1st and 2nd set "MIOJ"..$10.00 – 12.50
3rd set MB in wreath..$10.00 – 12.50
4th set "Sanjo China" ....$12.50 – 15.00
5th set "MIOJ" ....$15.00 – 17.50

Page 40

Top Row:
1st set "OJ" ....$10.00 – 12.50
2nd set "Ucagco China" ....$10.00 – 12.50
3rd set "OJ," "W" in wreath ....$15.00 – 17.50
4th set ....$10.00 – 12.50

2nd Row:
1st set "Ucagco China" ....$12.50 – 15.00
2nd set "Ucagco China" ....$12.50 – 15.00
3rd set (red)..$10.00 – 12.50
4th set (red)..$10.00 – 12.50

3rd Row:
1st set (red)..$10.00 – 12.50
2nd set (red) ....$10.00 – 12.50
3rd set (red) ....$10.00 – 12.50
4th set "Ucagco China".......................................$12.50 – 15.00

4th Row:
1st set "OJ" ....$10.00 – 12.50

2nd set (orange)..$10.00 – 12.50
3rd set "Trimont China".......................................$17.50 – 20.00
4th set "Meito Norleans China," "Livonia"................$10.00 – 12.50

5th Row:
1st set "Merit," "OJ" ....$12.50 – 15.00
2nd set (blue)...$8.00 – 10.00
3rd set "Ucagco China" ....$15.00 – 17.50
4th set (orange) ....$10.00 – 12.50

Page 42

Top Row:
Celluloid Reindeer, 7" x 7½".................................$12.50 – 15.00
Santa Planter, 5½" x 6"......................................$25.00 – 27.50
Tree, w/Bulbs, 6¼..$7.50 – 10.00

2nd Row:
Skier, 3½"...$25.00 – 30.00
2nd, 3rd, and 4th Ornaments, 3½" ....$6.00 – 7.50
Holly Leaf, 4" w/wire attachments ....$3.00 – 3.50 ea.
Santa Pipe Cleaner, 4" ....$15.00 – 20.00
Santa Ornament, 4" ....$22.50 – 25.00

3rd Row:
Nativity Set, 7 piece, 2½".....................................$35.00 – 40.00

4th and 5th Rows:
Nativity Set in paper maché
    (missing Christ Child)..$125.00 – 150.00 set

Page 44

Column 1: (Vertically)
Box of 12 Bells, "MIOJ" on box No. 51....................$30.00 – 35.00
Box of 12 Ornaments, each 3¼" long.........................$30.00 – 35.00

Column 2:
Box of 12 Ornaments, each 3¼" long, "MIOJ" ....$30.00 – 35.00
Box of 12 various designs each 2" long, "MIOJ"........$17.50 – 20.00
"Christmas Tree Ornaments," 1 Doz. ....$12.50 – 15.00
"Glass Ball Ornaments," 1 Doz., Maker "MIOJ"........$12.50 – 15.00

Page 46

Top Row:
Cup and Saucer Wall Plaque 3¼"............................$6.00 – 7.50
Flower Bowl, "Pico"..$8.00 – 10.00
Snack Plate, 9" leaf, "Shofu China" ....$8.00 – 10.00
Match Safe, 6¼"..$35.00 – 37.50

2nd Row:
Plate, 5" ....$6.00 – 7.50
Plate, 4½", Ardalt...$6.00 – 7.50
Children's Vases, 2" pr. ....$15.00 – 20.00

3rd Row:
Bowl, 7" ....$12.50 – 15.00
Plate, 6⅜", "Shozan"..$10.00 – 12.50
Hanging Planter w/24" pottery chain, "Marumon" .....$50.00 – 65.00

4th Row:
Bowl, 5¾" "Ucagco" ....$8.00 – 10.00
Handled Leaf Plate, 5½" ....$10.00 – 12.50
Handled Plate, 5¾" ....$12.50 – 15.00

Page 48

Top Row:
Plates, 8¼", "Rosetti" ....$20.00 – 22.50 ea.
"Cup of Gold," "Hibiscus," "Hybrid Cattelya"

2nd Row:
Handled Divided Tray, 10", Elephant head mark ....$10.00 – 12.50
2nd and 3rd Plates, 3¼", souvenir ....$5.00 – 6.00 ea.
4th Plate, 3⅜", souvenir ....$5.00 – 6.00
Flower Frog w/seven holes, 4½" ....$10.00 – 12.50

3rd Row:
Bowl, 6" ....$10.00 – 12.50
Plate, 7¾", "Ardalt" ....$20.00 – 25.00
Plate, 8" ....$65.00 – 75.00
Bowl, 6" ....$10.00 – 12.50

4th Row:
Leaf, 6½", "Ucagco China" ....$8.00 – 10.00
Leaf, 3", "Kyokuto China" ....$4.00 – 5.00
Leaf, 5½", "Chubu China" ....$10.00 – 12.50

5th Row:
Plates, 6⅛", "SGK China," "Andrea" ....$20.00 – 25.00 ea.

Page 50

Bowl, 5¾", cereal ....$6.00 – 7.50
Bowl, 8⅞", soup...$7.50 – 9.00
Bowl, 7¾" x 12", w/handles, casserole.....................$35.00 – 40.00
Creamer..$12.50 – 15.00
Cup...$10.00 – 12.50
Gravy Boat..$15.00 – 17.50
Gravy Platter, 9¼" ....$10.00 – 12.50
Plate, 6½" bread and butter ....$3.50 – 4.00
Plate, 7⅝", salad..$5.00 – 6.50
Plate, 10½", dinner...$12.50 – 15.00
Platter, 13½" ....$15.00 – 17.50
Platter, 18¼" ....$25.00 – 30.00
Saucer, 6½"..$2.00 – 2.50
Sugar w/Cover ....$17.50 – 20.00
Set for 4 including: cups, saucers, plates in 3 sizes, cereal and soup
    bowls, creamer and covered sugar ....$175.00 – 200.00
Set for 6 including all of the items listed above for 6 and gravy
    boat and platter..$225.00 – 250.00
Set for 8 including all of above for 8 & small platter ..$275.00 – 300.00
Set for 12 including all of above for 12 and adding casserole
    and large platter..$400.00 – 450.00

Page 52

Bowl, 5½", cereal...$6.00 – 7.50
Bowl, 7½", soup...$8.00 – 10.00
Bowl, 7½" x 11", oval..$15.00 – 17.50
Creamer..$10.00 – 12.50
Cup...$10.00 – 12.50
Gravy Boat..$15.00 – 17.50
Gravy Platter, 9¼" ....$10.00 – 12.50
Plate, 6⅝", bread and butter ....$3.00 – 4.50
Plate, 7⅝", salad..$5.00 – 6.50
Plate, 10¾", dinner...$12.50 – 15.00
Platter, 12¼" ....$17.50 – 20.00
Saucer...$2.00 – 2.50
Sugar w/Cover ....$15.00 – 17.50

Set for 4 including: cups, saucers, plates in 3 sizes, cereal
    and soup bowls, creamer and covered sugar ....$175.00 – 200.00
Set for 6 including all of the items listed above for 6 and gravy
    boat and platter..$225.00 – 250.00
Set for 8 including all of above for 8 and
    small platter..$275.00 – 300.00

Page 54

Bowl, 5¾", cereal..$6.00 – 7.50
Bowl, 8⅛", soup..$8.00 – 10.00
Bowl, 10", round vegetable ....$15.00 – 17.50
Bowl, 10¾", oval vegetable ....$17.50 – 20.00
Creamer..$10.00 – 12.50
Cup...$10.00 – 12.50
Gravy Boat w/Attached Platter ....$22.50 – 25.00
Plate, 6⅜", bread and butter ....$3.50 – 4.00
Plate, 7¾", salad..$6.00 – 7.50
Plate, 10", dinner..$12.00 – 13.50
Platter, 14¼" ....$20.00 – 22.50
Saucer...$2.00 – 2.50
Sugar w/Cover (cover not shown) ....$12.50 – 15.00
Set for 4 including: cups, saucers, plates in 3 sizes, cereal
    and soup bowls, creamer and covered sugar........$200.00 – 225.00
Set for 6 including all of above
    for 6 and gravy and platter attached....................$250.00 – 275.00
Set for 8 including all of above
    for 8 with platter and vegetable bowls.................$325.00 – 350.00
Set for 12 including all of above
    for 12 with additional serving pieces ....$450.00 – 500.00

Page 56

Top Row:
Plate, 10" "Empire Shape, Meito China, Ivory China"..$8.00 – 10.00
Demitasse Cup and Saucer, "Highmount"......................$6.00 – 8.00
Plate, 7½", "Hira China"...$6.00 – 8.00
Plate, 10", "Empire Shape, Meito China, Dexter,
    Ivory China"...$7.00 – 9.00
Cup, "Merit China" ....$6.00 – 7.50

2nd Row:
Demitasse Cup and Saucer..$6.00 – 8.00
"Blue Willow" Cup and Saucer ....$15.00 – 20.00
"Blue Willow" Bowl, 5", ...$7.50 – 10.00
"Blue Willow" Egg Cup, 3¾"..$20.00 – 22.50

3rd Row:
Plate, 5⅝", marked K in circle ....$8.00 – 10.00
Demitasse Cup and Saucer, "Ucagco China" ....$8.00 – 10.00
Plate, 7½" (same as 1st) ....$10.00 – 12.50
Sugar, (same as 1st)....................$12.50 w/o lid, 15.00 – 17.50 w/lid

4th Row:
Platter, 10" x 14", "Ironstone Ware" ....$25.00 – 27.50
"Blue Willow" Child's Tureen, 5" x 2¾" ....$40.00 – 45.00

Page 58

Top Row:
Black Fiddler, 5" ....$40.00 – 42.50
Black Fiddler, 6" ....$50.00 – 55.00
Indian Squaw, 4½" ....$10.00 – 12.50
Indian (Asian), 6" ....$12.50 – 15.00
Balloon Lady, 5½" ....$45.00 – 50.00

24

Indian w/Papoose, 5½" ....$20.00 – 22.50
Indian Planter, 3" ....$8.00 – 10.00
Indian Chief, 5½" ....$22.50 – 25.00
Indian Squaw, 6" ....$30.00 – 35.00

2nd Row:
Black Band Members, 2¾" ....$20.00 – 22.50 ea.
Chinese Couple, 5¼" ....$20.00 – 22.50
Buddha, 5½" ....$20.00 – 22.50
Incense Burner, 4" ....$20.00 – 22.50
Dancer, 5" ....$22.50 – 25.00
Black Shoeshine Boy, 5½" ....$45.00 – 50.00

3rd Row:
Religious Symbols, 4" to 4¾" ....$6.50 ea. or 47.50 – 50.00 set

4th Row:
Dutch Water Girl, 4" ....$10.00 – 12.50
Dutch Planter, 3", "Pico" ....$12.50 – 15.00
3rd and 5th Delft Ladies, 6¼" ....$32.50 – 35.00 ea.
Dutch Girl w/Milk Can, 6" ....$20.00 – 22.50
Dutch Children, 3" ....$10.00 – 12.50 ea.
Dutch Egg Timer w/Sand Timer 3½" complete ....$20.00 – 22.50

5th Row:
Eskimos, 3" and 2¾" ....$12.50 – 15.00 ea.
Indian Water Boy, 4" ....$10.00 – 12.00
Indian, 3" ....$8.00 – 10.00
Spanish Guitar Player, 4¼" ....$8.00 – 10.00
Mexican 5¼" ....$17.50 – 20.00
Martian (?), 3" ....$20.00 – 25.00
Indian Canoe w/Plastic Flowers.....................$18.00 – 20.00

Page 60
Top Row:
Couple at Piano, 4" ....$20.00 – 22.50
Dancing Couple, 4½" ....$18.00 – 20.00
Triple, 3" ....$12.50 – 15.00
Romantic Couple, 4" ....$20.00 – 22.50
Couple, 4½", "Canadian National Exhibition, Toronto,
    Canada"..$17.50 – 20.00
Couple, 4" ....$12.50 – 15.00

2nd Row:
1st and 4th Serenading Couple, 5¼" and 5⅛" ....$18.00 – 20.00 ea.
Coach et. al., 5¾" x 7" ....$65.00 – 75.00
Serenading Couple, 4½" ....$15.00 – 17.50
Triple w/Piano, 3¾" ....$25.00 – 27.50

3rd Row:
Couple Waiting for Rain, 5½" "Highmount" ....$22.50 – 25.00
2nd and 3rd Couples, 5½" and 5¼" ....$18.00 – 20.00 ea.
4th, 5th, and 6th Couples, 4¼" to 3¾" ....$12.50 – 15.00 ea.
Couple, 4½" ....$15.00 – 17.50

4th Row:
1st, 3rd, and 4th Couples, 6⅞" to 6⅜" ....$30.00 – 35.00 ea.
Musicians, 7" x 7⅞", Villain and Captive, 7½" ....$50.00 – 55.00 ea.

Page 62
Top Row:
Dancers, 5" ....$15.00 ea. or 35.00 – 37.50 pr.

Robed in Red, 6⅛" ....$20.00 ea. or 42.50 – 45.00 pr.
Pair, 5⅞" and 6" ....$20.00 ea. or 42.50 – 45.00 pr.
Pair, 6½" and 6" ....$22.50 ea. or 47.50 – 50.00 pr.

2nd Row:
1st & 2nd pairs are all marked the same, 4½" $10.00 ea. or 20.00 – 22.50 pr.
"It was this long", 4¼" ....$10.00 ea. or 20.00 – 22.50 pr.
Musicians, 4½" ....$12.50 ea. or 25.00 – 30.00 pr.

3rd Row:
Dancers, 7½" ....$22.50 ea. or 47.50 – 50.00 pr.
Dancers, 8⅛" ....$30.00 ea. or 62.50 – 65.00 pr.
Couple, 7¾" and 8" ....$30.00 ea. or 62.50 – 65.00 pr.

4th Row
Couple, 7½" and 7⅜", "Mariyama" ....$20.00 ea. or 40.00 – 45.00 pr.
Dancers, 8¾" ....$42.50 ea. or 90.00 – 100.00 pr.
Prayerful Couple, 7⅝", "Mariyama"........$17.50 ea. or 35.00 – 40.00 pr.

Page 64
Top Row:
Grandfather, 6" ....$25.00 – 27.50
Warrior, 8" ....$35.00 – 40.00
Girl w/Bird, 6" ....$22.50 – 25.00
Girl, 7⅛" ....$25.00 – 27.50
5th and 7th, Coolie and Musician, 7" and 6½" ....$22.50 – 25.00 ea.
Holding Flowers, 6" ....$20.00 – 22.50

2nd Row:
Lady w/Flowers, 5½" ....$18.00 – 20.00
Bended Knee Flower Offering, 5" ....$18.00 – 20.00
3rd and 5th Musician and Lady, 5" ....$15.00 – 17.50 ea.
Girl w/Bow, 4½" ....$12.50 – 15.00

3rd Row:
Instrument Player, 9" ....$40.00 – 45.00
Lady w/Muff, 8" ....$30.00 – 32.50
Musician, 10" ....$60.00 – 65.00
Warrior, 8¼" ....$35.00 – 37.50
Robed Man, 8" ....$32.50 – 35.00
Woman, 7½" ....$25.00 – 27.50

4th Row:
Lady w/Fan, 5", Baldy, 4" ....$15.00 – 17.50 ea.
Coolie, 3¼" ....$10.00 – 12.50
Coolie, 4" ....$12.50 – 15.00
Man w/Rabbits, 4" ....$35.00 – 40.00
Lady w/Fan, 3¾" ....$32.50 – 35.00
Dancer, 4½" ....$18.00 – 20.00

Page 66
Top Row:
Double Pair, 6"..$30.00 ea. or 62.50 – 65.00 pr.
Courting Couple Double, 6" ....$55.00 ea. or 115.00 – 125.00 pr.

2nd Row:
Busts, 5½" ....$17.50 ea. or 37.50 – 40.00 pr.
Trio, 4" and 3¾" ....$12.50 – 15.00 ea.
Seated Couple, 5½" ....$40.00 ea. or 85.00 – 90.00 pr.

3rd Row:
Double, 4¾" ....$12.50 ea. or 27.50 – 30.00 pr.

Musician and Friend, 5" ....$15.00 ea. or 32.50 – 35.00 pr.
Couple, 5" ....$10.00 ea. or 22.50 – 25.00 pr.

4th Row:
Flower Holders, 7" ....$30.00 ea. or 65.00 – 75.00 pr.
Shepherds, 13½" ....$75.00 ea. or 160.00 – 175.00 pr.
Dancers, 6¼" and 6" ....$20.00 ea. or 42.50 – 45.00 pr.
White Dancers, 6¼" ....$15.00 ea. or 32.50 – 35.00 pr.

Page 68

Top Row:
1st, 2nd, and 3rd Ladies, 4" ....$10.00 – 12.00 ea.
4th, 5th, and 6th Dancers, 3¾" and 4" ....$12.50 – 15.00 ea.
Ballerina, 4½" ....$22.50 – 25.00
Ballerina, 5¾" ....$35.00 – 40.00

2nd Row:
1st, 3rd, and 4th Figures, 5¼" and 5" ....$18.00 – 20.00 ea.
2nd Cellist, 3¼" ....$12.50 – 15.00
5th and 7th Figurines, 4¼" ....$12.50 – 15.00 ea.
6th Figure, 4" ....$10.00 – 12.00

3rd Row:
Lady, 5" ....$18.00 – 20.00
2nd, 6th, and 8th Ladies, 4¾" and 5" ....$12.50 – 15.00 ea.
3rd and 5th Flower Ladies, 5" and 5¾" ....$15.00 – 17.50 ea.
4th and 7th Ladies, 4" and 4¼" ....$10.00 – 12.50 ea.

4th Row:
1st and 11th Figurines, 7" and 6¼" ....$22.50 – 25.00 ea.
2nd, 4th, and 8th Flower Ladies, 4¼" and 4" ...$10.00 – 12.50 ea.
3rd Mandolin Player, 10¼" ....$45.00 – 50.00
5th Lady, 12¼" ....$65.00 – 75.00
6th Windy Flower Girl, 5" ....$15.00 – 17.50
7th and 9th Ladies, 7" and 6¾" ....$27.50 – 30.00 ea.
10th Peddler, 3½" ....$8.00 – 10.00

Page 70

Top Row:
Man with Hat, 7¼" ....$27.50 – 30.00
2nd and 3rd Men, 8" ....$35.00 – 40.00 ea.
Man, 7½" ....$27.50 – 30.00
Seated, 6¼" ....$22.50 – 25.00

2nd Row:
Man with Flowers, 5" ....$15.00 – 17.50
2nd, 5th, and 6th Men, 4" ....$12.50 – 15.00 ea.
3rd Man, 3" ....$8.00 – 10.00
4th Man, 3½" ....$8.00 – 10.00
7th Waver, 5½" ....$18.00 – 20.00

3rd Row:
1st and 2nd Men, 6" and 6½" ....$27.50 – 30.00 ea.
Bottle Boy, 5¼" ....$18.00 – 20.00
4th and 5th Men, 6½" and 6" ....$20.00 – 22.50 ea.
Violinist, 5⅜" ....$12.50 – 15.00

4th Row:
1st and 5th Men, 8" and 7½" ....$35.00 – 37.50 ea.
Uniformed Man, 10⅜" ....$60.00 – 65.00
Colonial, 10" ....$65.00 – 75.00
Red Head, 9¾" ....$65.00 – 75.00

Page 72

Top Row:
1st to 4th Stemware, 4¼" to 5¼" ....$15.00 – 17.50 ea.

2nd Row:
Pink Atomizer ....$22.50 – 25.00
Blue Atomizer ....$27.50 – 30.00
Perfume Set...$45.00 – 50.00 set
Blue Cologne and Atomizer on blue tray ....$50.00 – 55.00 set

3rd Row:
Blue Atomizer ....$25.00 – 27.50
Animals w/Paper Stickers ....$6.00 – 7.50 ea.

4th Row:
Parrot Lamp ....$75.00 – 85.00
Crystal Perfume and Stopper ....$20.00 – 22.50
Green Pair of Atomizers ....$27.50 ea. or 57.50 – 60.00 pr.

5th Row:
Perfume, pink or green......................................$17.50 – 20.00 ea.
Blue Perfume and green or blue ....$20.00 – 22.50 ea.
Pink Perfume...$22.50 – 25.00
Blue Perfume w/Unusual Stopper......................$25.00 – 30.00

Page 74

Top Row:
Wood Cigarette Box, 3½" x 5" ....$35.00 – 40.00
Wooden Jewelry Box, 7½" x 7¾" ....$65.00 – 75.00
Bead String, 60" long..$25.00 – 30.00
Chest, 2 drawer, 3" x 4½" ....$20.00 – 22.50

2nd Row:
Crochet Purse, 5" x 8½".....................................$60.00 – 75.00
Wooden Box, 4" x 7" ....$30.00 – 35.00
Butterfly Brooches ....$1.50 – 2.00 ea.
Bead Purse, 7" x 7½" ....$60.00 – 75.00

3rd Row:
Geisha Dancer Music Box, 12" x 5" ....$150.00 – 175.00
Rosary Beads, 30"..$30.00 – 35.00
Pearls, 16"..$30.00 – 35.00
Harmonica Bracelet, 7½" ....$20.00 – 22.50
Pearl Bracelet...$18.00 – 20.00
Gold Expansion Bracelet ....$20.00 – 22.50
Purple Beads, 24"..$18.00 – 20.00

Page 76

Top Row:
Lady, 6"...$40.00 – 50.00
Corner Shelf, 9¼" ....$40.00 – 45.00
Chest, 3" x 4¼" ....$35.00 – 40.00

2nd Row:
Coaster, 4¼"...$3.50 – 4.00 ea.
Box, 5" x 2"..$27.50 – 30.00 set
Dancer, 4¼" ....$25.00 – 30.00
Box Set of Coasters..$27.50 – 30.00 set
Coaster, 4¼" for set..$3.50 – 4.00 ea.

3rd Row:
Relish, 3-part, 5¾" x 15" ....$55.00 – 60.00

Wooden Coaster Box and six 2¾" Coasters ....$25.00 – 30.00 set

4th Row:
Salt Box, 5" x 5" ....$50.00 – 60.00
Corner Shelf, 13¾" ....$65.00 – 75.00
Dancer, 4" ....$20.00 – 25.00
Wooden Clothes Hanger, 10" x 10"..................$22.50 – 25.00
Wood Salad Bowl, 10"..$15.00 – 17.50
Wood Salad Bowl, 6"...$6.00 – 7.50 ea.

Page 78

Top Row:
1st and 2nd Double Pair, 11" ....$30.00 ea. or 65.00 – 70.00 pr.
3rd Couple, 10½" ....$30.00 – 32.50
4th Couple, 10½" ....$32.50 – 35.00
5th Male Bouquet Holder, 10" ....$27.50 – 30.00
6th Lady's Head, 10" ....$50.00 – 55.00

2nd Row:
1st and 2nd Double Pair, 10½" ....$30.00 ea. or 65.00 – 70.00 pr.
3rd Musician and Singer, 11½" ....$30.00 – 32.50
4th Dancing Couple, 11½" ....$45.00 – 50.00
5th Courting Couple, 10" ....$32.50 – 35.00

3rd Row:
1st and 2nd Pair, 11" ....$50.00 ea. or 105.00 – 115.00 pr.
2nd, 3rd and 4th Couples, 10" and 11½" ....$35.00 – 40.00 ea.

Page 80

Top Row:
"Fleur de lis" design, four 10" square napkins and one 32"
    square tablecloth ....$75.00 – 85.00 set

2nd Row:
Damask set of four 12" square napkins and one 48" x 52"
    tablecloth...$85.00 – 100.00 set

3rd Row:
Linen set of four 10½" napkins and one 32" square
    tablecloth...$80.00 – 90.00 set

4th Row:
Tablecloth, 48" square ....$40.00 – 50.00
Tablecloth, 50" x 50" ....$35.00 – 45.00
Four Damask Napkins, 12½" square........$12.00 ea. or 50.00 – 52.50 set

5th Row:
Embroidered Towels 13" x 17"...............$20.00 – 22.50 ea.
Peach Tablecloth and Napkin Set ....$75.00 – 85.00 set
Napkins, 12½" square ....$10.00 – 12.00 ea.

Page 82

Vertically By Column
Column 1 Top:
Butler, 5¼" x 6" ....$8.00 – 10.00
Copper Butler, souvenir of Washington, D. C..............$8.00 – 10.00
Butler, NY souvenir ....$12.00 – 15.00
Crumb Butler ....$6.00 – 7.50
Crumb Butler, souvenir of Washington, D. C. ....$5.00 – 6.50

Column 2 Top:
Tray, 9½" x 4½"..$7.50 – 9.00

Tray, 4¾" x 2", United Nations souvenir.......................$8.00 – 10.00
Golden Tray, 4¼" x 5¾" ....$6.00 – 7.50
Ash Tray, 4¾" Souvenir of N.Y.C............................$12.50 – 15.00

Column 3:
Turtle Wind-Up Toy ....$20.00 – 25.00
Puzzles w/mirror on back, 2¼" (Clown, Dog, Cat) ....$8.00 – 10.00 ea.

Column 4 Top:
Ash Tray, N.Y.C. souvenir ....$10.00 – 12.50
Heart Trays Souvenirs of Canada and New Orleans ......$6.00 – 7.50 ea.
Trays, 5" 3½", souvenirs of New Mexico and
    Washington, D. C...$5.00 – 6.50 ea.

Page 84

Top Row:
Covered Sugar, 2¼" x 5" ....$10.00 – 12.50
Creamer to match...$5.00 – 7.50
Candlesticks, 5" pair ....$22.50 – 25.00
Jewel Box, 2" to 3½" ....$8.00 – 10.00
Jewel Box, 2½" x 3½" ....$10.00 – 12.50

2nd Row:
Scotty Dog Covered Box, 2½" x 3½" ....$12.50 – 15.00
Mini Teapot, Creamer, Covered Sugar on Tray, 4".....$22.50 – 25.00
Covered Butter, 3¼" x 4½"..$15.00 – 17.50
Salt and Pepper Shakers, 1⅜" ....$10.00 – 12.50
Jewel Box, 3" x 3½" ....$12.50 – 15.00
Creamer and Sugar on 7¾" Tray ....$22.50 – 25.00 set

3rd Row:
Salt & Pepper Shakers, 2¼"...$15.00 – 17.50
Cigarette Urns, 3" ....$7.50 – 8.50 ea.
Covered Sugar...$12.50 – 15.00
Jewel Box, deer on top..$12.50 – 15.00
Jewel Box, horse on top..$15.00 – 17.50
Tea Strainer ....$10.00 – 12.50

4th Row:
Buddhas, 2⅛" ....$8.00 – 10.00 ea.
Crown Box, 3" x 3½"...$15.00 – 17.50
Niagara Falls Souvenir Piano Box ....$17.50 – 20.00
"Pico" Piano Box ....$17.50 – 20.00
Salt & Pepper, 3" souvenir of Niagara Falls................$15.00 – 17.50

5th Row:
Souvenir Ash Trays...$3.00 – 3.50 ea.
Special Trays ....$8.00 – 10.00 ea.

Page 86

Top Row:
Jewel Box, 3½" x 4½" ....$12.50 – 15.00
2nd and 4th Vase, 8"..32.50 – 35.00 pr.
3rd Vase, 7"...$15.00 – 17.50
Cigarette Box, 3½" x 4¼" ....$18.00 – 20.00

2nd Row:
1st and 3rd Sugar and Creamer on 7½" Tray..............$22.50 – 25.00 ea.
2nd Miniature Set in 4" Tray ....$15.00 – 17.50

3rd Row:
Horse and Sulky ....$25.00 – 27.50

Salt and Pepper on Tray, 5⅜" ....$25.00 – 27.50
Handled Candlestick ....$22.50 – 25.00 pr.

4th Row:
1st and 2nd Piano Jewel Boxes, 2½ " x 3"..................$15.00 – 17.50 ea.
Bowl, 6¼" ....$8.00 – 10.00
Piano Box, 2¼" x 3½" ....$15.00 – 17.50
Cowboy Boot ....$6.00 – 7.50

5th Row:
Dragon Covered Box, 4" x 7" ....$25.00 – 27.50
Salt and pepper on tray ....$17.50 – 20.00
Jewel Box, w/Lock, 3¾" x 6¾" ....$25.00 – 27.50

Page 88

Top Row:
Bookends, 4½" x 5½" ....$17.50 ea. or 35.00 – 40.00 pr.
Candleholders, 4" ....$22.50 ea. or 50.00 – 55.00 pr.
Elf on Snail, 4¼" ....$27.50 – 30.00

2nd Row:
Purple Elf, reclining ....$12.50 – 15.00
Green Elf, sitting ....$15.00 – 17.50
Colonial Lady Double Candleholder, 4".................$20.00 – 22.50
Colonial Lady Single Candleholder, 4" ....$17.50 – 20.00

3rd Row:
Accordion Playing Elf, 3¼" ....$15.00 – 17.50
Lady Bell, 3" ....$22.50 – 25.00
Chef Bell, 3" ....$22.50 – 25.00
Mushroom Elves, 1⅝" ....$10.00 – 12.50
Elephant Bank, 2¼" x 3¾".....................................$25.00 – 30.00

4th Row:
Clown, 4" ....$12.50 – 15.00
Clown, 4½" ....$20.00 – 25.00
Powder Jar Lady, 5¾"...$35.00 – 40.00
Clown, 6¼" ....$22.50 – 25.00
Bookend Pair, 4" x 5½" ....$17.50 ea. or 37.50 – 40.00 pr.

5th Row:
Blue Powder Jar, 2½" ....$8.00 – 10.00
Heart Powder Jar, 2¾" ....$10.00 – 12.50
Lady in Swing Powder Jar, 7½" ....$50.00 – 60.00
Blue Heart, 2¼" ....$8.00 – 10.00
Blue w/Rose Powder, 3½" ....$12.50 – 15.00
"Wedgwood"-type Box, 3¼" x 2" ....$15.00 – 17.50

Page 90

Top Row:
Silk Scarf, 48" x 18½" ....$45.00 – 50.00
Baby Sweater ....$40.00 – 45.00
Cat Pin Cushion, 3½" x 5¼" ....$12.50 – 15.00

2nd Row:
Organdy Crewel Scarf, 11" x 5¼" ....$18.00 – 20.00

3rd Row:
Lamp Scarves, 10¾" square.....................................$25.00 – 27.50 ea.

4th Row:
Celluloid Tape Measure, 3" girl...............................$15.00 – 17.50

Heart Box ....$4.00 – 5.00
Sewing Kit ....$18.00 – 20.00
Picture ....$45.00 – 50.00

Page 92

Top Row:
Box, 2⅞" ....$5.00 – 6.00
Lady's Slipper, 2¾" ....$6.00 – 7.50
Shoe, 2¾" ....$3.00 – 3.50
Shoe House, 4"..$10.00 – 12.50
Baby Shoe, 3⅝" x 2⅜" ....$6.00 – 7.50
Brown and White Shoe, 3" ....$3.00 – 3.50
Shoe, 2½" ....$4.00 – 5.00
Vase, 3⅛" ....$6.00 – 7.50

2nd Row:
Water Sprinkling Can, 2¾" ....$2.50 – 3.00
Wheelbarrow, 3½" ....$3.00 – 3.50
Shoe, 3½" ....$4.00 – 5.00
Pitcher Vase, 3⅛" ....$2.50 – 3.00
Valise, 2⅛" ....$3.00 – 3.50
Pitcher, 3½" ....$8.00 – 10.00
Basket, 3" ....$5.00 – 6.00
Wooden Rickshaw, 3½" ....$15.00 – 17.50
Pitcher, Vase, 3½" ....$8.00 – 10.00

3rd Row:
Blue Pitcher, 2½" ....$3.00 – 3.50
Pitcher, 2½" ....$2.50 – 3.00
Teapot and Lid, 2¼" ....$4.00 – 5.00
Wells, 1⅜" ....$2.50 – 3.00 ea.
Bamboo House, 2½" ....$6.00 – 7.50
Lighthouse, 2⅝" ....$2.50 – 3.00
Horse-drawn Wagon, 4" ....$6.00 – 7.50
Car, 5" ....$10.00 – 12.50
Goose and Basket, 1¾" ....$4.00 – 5.00

4th Row:
Small Items ....$2.00 – 3.00 ea.
Larger Items ....$4.00 – 5.00 ea.
Mermaid, 3½" ....$22.50 – 25.00
Castle, 3½" x 5½" ....$12.50 – 15.00
Cat w/Fish, 4¼" ....$17.50 – 20.00

5th Row:
Covered Urn, 2½" ....$6.00 – 7.50
Leaf, 2½" ....$4.00 – 5.00
Egg Cup, 2¼" ....$7.50 – 9.00
Pitcher, 3¼" ....$3.00 – 3.50
Wheelbarrow, 2" ....$2.50 – 3.00
Easter Basket, 7" x 7" ....$30.00 – 35.00
Flowerpot, 4½" ....$8.00 – 10.00
Vase, 2" ....$2.50 – 3.00
Pitcher, 2½" ....$3.00 – 3.50
Souvenir Pitcher, 2½" ....$3.00 – 3.50
Souvenir Pitcher, 3" ....$3.00 – 3.50

Page 94

Top Row:
Umbrella, 18" ....$25.00 – 27.50
Umbrella, 22" ....$27.50 – 30.00

2nd Row:
Party Horns, 12¼"..$6.00 – 7.50
Paper Lantern, 4¼"..$10.00 – 12.50
Needles, 50 asst..$15.00 – 17.50

3rd Row:
Orange Fan, 7¾" spine...$10.00 – 12.50
Blue Fan, 8¾"...$12.50 – 15.00
Party Favor..$12.50 – 15.00

4th Row:
Satin Flower Bunch..$12.50 – 15.00
Pink and Blue Fan, 8½"..$10.00 – 12.50
Fan, 13¼"..$25.00 – 30.00
Pink Flower Bunch, 8½"..$8.00 – 10.00
Flower Fan, 8½"..$15.00 – 17.50

5th Row:
Pink Poseys, 4¼"..$7.50 – 8.00
Flag, 1⅞"...$4.00 – 5.00
Needle Assortment...$10.00 – 12.50
Party Foldout 6"..$6.00 – 7.50
String Bowl, 5¾"..$20.00 – 25.00

Page 96

Top Row:
Swan, 4" x 5½"...$20.00 – 25.00
Duck, 3½" x 6"...$12.50 – 15.00
Duck, 3" x 5"...$10.00 – 12.50

2nd Row:
Goose, 3½"..$5.00 – 6.00
Bird on Tree Branch, 3"..$12.50 – 15.00 ea.
Rooster w/Cart, 3" x 4½"..$6.00 – 7.50
Birds in Tree, 3¼" x 4½"...$15.00 – 17.50

3rd Row:
Duck w/Scarf, 3¼" x 4"..$8.00 – 10.50
Owl 2½"..$8.00 – 10.00
Swan, 2"...$3.00 – 3.50
Duck w/Cart, 3" x 5"...$6.00 – 7.50
Donald Duck, 3"...$12.50 – 15.00

4th Row:
Swan, 3"...$5.00 – 6.00
Parrot, 6¼"..$18.00 – 20.00
Duck w/Hat, 6½" x 6"..$10.00 – 12.50
Duck Held by Child, 4"...$12.50 – 15.00

5th Row:
Bird w/House 3"..$6.00 – 7.50
Birds on Flowers of Branch, 3½" x 4½"....................$12.50 – 15.00 ea.
Flamingo, 3"...$15.00 – 17.50

Page 98

Top Row:
Rabbit w/Cart, 2½" x 6"..$12.50 – 15.00
Elephant, 2"...$6.00 – 7.50
Elephant, 3½" x 5"..$12.50 – 15.00
Pig, 2"..$6.00 – 7.50
Lamb, 3"...$5.00 – 6.00

2nd Row:
Monkey Clown, 3¾"...$10.00 – 12.50
Rabbit w/Cart, 4" x 4"..$15.00 – 17.50
Zebra, 5¼" x 6¼"..$10.00 – 12.50
Ox w/Cart, 2½" x 7"..$8.00 – 10.00

3rd Row:
Donkey, 2¾"...$6.00 – 7.50
Dog w/Cart, 1¾"...$4.00 – 5.00
Dog, 2⅞"...$4.00 – 5.00
Dog w/Shoe, 2"...$6.00 – 7.50
Dogw/Basket, 2"...$4.00 – 5.00

4th Row:
Frog, 2¼"...$8.00 – 10.00
Dog, 4¾"...$12.50 – 15.00
Dog w/Master, 5"..$12.50 – 15.00
Dog, 4" x 6½"...$10.00 – 12.50
Bear on Log, 3½"..$6.00 – 7.50

5th Row:
Cat w/Slipper, 2½" x 5¼".......................................$10.00 – 12.50
Dog, 2¾"...$3.00 – 4.00
Cow, 3" x 4"...$8.00 – 10.00
Bug with Bonnet, 4" x 4½"......................................$10.00 – 12.50

Page 100

Top Row:
Boy at Cactus, 4"..$6.00 – 7.50
Girl w/Fan, 6"...$12.50 – 15.00
Chinese Pair of Planters, 5"....................................$10.00 ea.
Chinese Pair of Planters, 5"....................................22.50 – 25.00 pr.
Seated Oriental, 4"..$7.50 – 9.00

2nd Row:
Dancers, 4½"..$15.00 – 17.50 ea.
Colonial Lady, 4"...$5.00 – 6.00
Oriental Lady Head, 4"...$12.50 – 15.00
Girl Pushing Cart, 4"...$10.00 – 12.50

3rd Row:
Boy w/Bird, 3"..$5.00 – 6.00
Couple, 2½"...$8.00 – 10.00
Boy w/Flowers, 2"...$3.00 – 4.00
Boy w/Horn, 3"...$8.00 – 10.00
Boy w/Guitar, 2¾"...$6.00 – 8.00
Dutch Girl w/Cart, 2¾"...$8.00 – 10.00

4th Row:
Girl w/White Dress, 7"..$18.00 – 20.00
Boy w/Hat, 5½"...$10.00 – 12.50
Coolie w/Basket, 6"...$10.00 – 12.50
Elf w/Cart, 7½"...$15.00 – 20.00
Oriental, 5½"..$15.00 – 17.50

5th Row:
Mexican w/Guitar, 4¼"...$15.00 – 17.50
Sleepy Mexican, 3½"..$10.00 – 12.50
Mandolin Player, 4"...$6.00 – 8.00
Boy w/Topknot, 4"...$12.50 – 15.00
Girl w/Basket, 4¾"..$10.00 – 12.50

Page 102

Top Row:
Colonial Couple, 6½" x 6" ....$42.50 – 45.00
Same as above only painted differently ....$42.50 – 45.00
Colonial Lady, 7" x 4¾" ....$27.50 – 30.00

2nd Row:
Colonial Couple, 6½" x 5¾" ....$35.00 ea. or 72.50 – 75.00 pr.
Dutch Boy, 7½" ....$20.00 – 25.00

3rd Row:
Couple w/Baskets, 6⅞" x 4¾" ....$45.00 ea. or 95.00 – 100.00 pr.
Monkeys, 5" ....$32.50 – 35.00 ea.

Page 104

Woven rug, 3' x 5' ....$50.00 – 60.00

Page 105

Top:
Wool hooked rug, 9' x 12' ....$300.00 – 400.00
Bottom:
Wool hooked rug, 4' x 6' ....$100.00 – 125.00

Page 106

Top Row:
Humpty Dumpty ....$55.00 – 60.00 pr.
Humpty Dumpty, small...................................$30.00 – 35.00 pr.
Mammy and Pappy ....$45.00 – 50.00

2nd Row:
Chicks in Basket ....$20.00 – 22.50
"Hummel"-type Children...................................$17.50 – 20.00
Chickens in Basket...$20.00 – 22.50
Mammy and Pappy ....$45.00 – 50.00

3rd Row:
Pigs...$15.00 – 17.50
Pigs in Sty ....$20.00 – 22.50
Dogs ....$12.50 – 15.00
Southern Belles ....$12.50 – 15.00

4th Row:
Indians..$15.00 – 17.50
Indians in Canoe ....$22.50 – 25.00
Fat Boy..$6.00 – 7.50
Boy w/Suspenders...$6.00 – 7.50
Duck Hugger..$7.00 – 8.50

5th Row:
Corn Cobs ....$10.00 – 12.50
Deer...$12.50 – 15.00
Pitchers on Tray ....$20.00 – 22.50

6th Row:
1st and 5th Geese pairs ....$15.00 – 17.50 ea pr.
2nd Duck...$10.00 – 12.50 pr.
3rd Ducks and 4th Geese pairs ....$12.50 – 15.00 ea pr.

Page 108

Top Row:
Baseball Players ....$22.50 – 25.00
Geisha Girls ....$20.00 – 22.50

Bellhop..$20.00 – 22.50
Coolies ....$27.50 – 30.00

2nd Row:
Graduates ....$18.00 – 20.00
Bride and Groom..$25.00 – 27.50
Scottish Couple ....$15.00 – 17.50
Dutch Girls ....$15.00 – 17.50

3rd Row:
Indian Zither Players......................................$15.00 – 17.50
Basket Children..$20.00 – 22.50
Lily of the Valley ....$12.50 – 15.00
Teakettles ....$10.00 – 12.50
Teakettle single ....$6.00 – 7.50

4th Row:
Cottage and Lighthouse ....$22.50 – 25.00
Children w/Animals ....$30.00 – 32.50
Glass Shakers on Tray ....$25.00 – 30.00

5th Row:
Glass on Metal Tray ....$17.50 – 20.00
Metal Shakers on Tray ....$15.00 – 17.50
Lady Mustard, Shakers, Spoon ....$35.00 – 40.00

Page 110

Top Row:
Three-piece Toby Set.......................................$75.00 – 90.00

2nd Row:
Windmill Sugar, 4" ....$15.00 – 17.50
Windmill Creamer, 3".......................................$8.00 – 10.00
Windmill Large Salt, 3"....................................$8.00 – 10.00
Windmill Teapot, 5" ....$35.00 – 40.00

3rd Row:
Salt, Pepper, and Marmalade on Tray........................$30.00 – 35.00
Salt, Pepper, and Mustard on Tray..........................$25.00 – 30.00
Sugar w/Lid..$15.00 – 17.50

4th Row:
Cookie Jar, 8" x 6¼" ....$65.00 – 75.00
Cottage Grease or Sugar ....$12.50 – 15.00
Biscuit Jar, 6½" x 5¼" ....$45.00 – 55.00

5th Row:
Bee Creamer, 2½" ....$10.00 – 12.50
Bee Teapot, 4½"..$30.00 – 35.00
Bee Sugar w/Lid, 3½".......................................$15.00 – 17.50

Page 112

Top Row:
Creamer..$8.00 – 10.00
Rice Bowl, 4"..$3.00 – 4.00
Bowl, 3"...$3.00 – 4.00
Rice Bowls, 4½" and 3½"....................................$4.00 – 5.00

2nd Row:
Saki Cups, 2¼"...$6.00 – 7.50 ea.
3rd to 5th and all of Row 3 ....$60.00 – 75.00 set

4th Row:
Demitasse Set for Six ....$50.00 – 55.00 set
2nd, 3rd, and 5th Saki Cups, 2¼" ....$6.00 – 7.50 ea.
Teapot, 6½" x 9" ....$18.00 – 20.00

Page 114

Top Row - Strawberry:
Sugar w/Lid and Creamer on Tray..............................$25.00 – 27.50 set
Salt, Pepper, Mustard w/Spoon ....$27.50 – 30.00 set

Second Row – Tomato:
Salt and Pepper, 3½" ....$15.00 – 17.50
Salt and Pepper, 3" ....$12.50 – 15.00
Sugar w/Lid..$12.50 – 15.00

3rd Row – Tomato:
Salt, Pepper, and Mustard ....$22.50 – 25.00 set
Teapot, 3" ....$30.00 – 35.00
Tumbler, 3" ....$10.00 – 12.50

4th Row – Tomato:
Teapot, 4½" ....$40.00 – 45.00
Teapot, 5½" ....$50.00 – 55.00
Tumbler as in Row 3

Fifth Row – Tomato:
Tumbler as in Row 3
Sugar w/Lid and Creamer ....$25.00 – 27.50
Salt, Pepper, and Mustard w/Spoon..........................$27.50 – 30.00 set

Page 116

Top Row:
Accordion Boy, 4" ....$12.50 – 15.00 ea.
Girl w/Bucket, 3" ....$10.00 – 12.50
Oriental Pair, 2¾" ....$12.50 ea. or 27.50 – 30.00 pr.
Fishing Couple, 2½" ....$15.00 – 17.50

2nd Row:
Musicians, 4½"...$12.50 ea. or 27.50 – 30.00 pr.
Oriental Musicians, 5" ....$15.00 ea. or 30.00 – 35.00 pr.
Fishing Couple 4" ....$17.50 – 20.00
Fishing Couple, 2¼" ....$10.00 – 12.50

3rd Row:
Boy with Basket, 4" ....$12.50 – 15.00
2nd and 4th Oriental Pair, 3".......................$8.50 ea. or 17.50 – 20.00 pr.
3rd and 5th Oriental Pair, 3¼" ....$10.00 ea. or 20.00 – 22.50 pr.
Cowboy Couple, 3½" and 3¾" ....$12.50 ea. or 27.50 – 30.00 pr.
Colonial Musicians, 3¼" ....$11.00 ea. or 22.50 – 25.00 pr.

4th Row:
1st and 6th Angels, 3" ....$20.00 ea. or 42.50 – 45.00 pr.
Girl and Doll, 5"..$17.50 – 20.00
Fishing Boy, 6½" ....$22.50 – 25.00
Ballerina, 5" ....$22.50 – 25.00
Mandolin Player, 4" ....$12.50 – 15.00

Page 118

Row 1 and Row 2 are "Wild Rose China"
Tea Set ....$135.00 – 150.00 set
Dinnerware Set for Eight ....$325.00 – 350.00

Row 3 and Row 4 are "Noritake"
Demitasse Set..$150.00 – 175.00 set

Page 120

Top Row:
Winker, 4" ....$22.50 – 25.00
Barrel, 4¼" ....$10.00 – 12.00
Cannibal Handled Mug, 4¼" ....$35.00 – 40.00

2nd Row:
Bearded Man, 2¾" ....$17.50 – 20.00
Colonial Man, 2¾" ....$15.00 – 17.50
3rd and 5th Colonial Lady, 2"..................$12.50 ea. or 27.50 – 30.00 pr.
Old Man, 1¾"..$12.50 – 15.00
Lady w/Basket, 2¼" ....$12.50 – 15.00
Lady w/Fork, 2¾" ....$15.00 – 17.50
Red Bearded Man, 2⅞" ....$17.50 – 20.00

3rd Row:
1st and 2nd Scarf Lady, 2½" ....$35.00 – 37.50 pr.
3rd Mustache Man, 2¼" ....$25.00 – 27.50
4th and 6th Lady, 2½" ....$20.00 – 22.50
5th Colonial Man, 3¼" ....$20.00 – 22.50

4th Row:
Stein, 6¾" ....$17.50 – 20.00
Stein, 7⅛" ....$20.00 – 22.50
Bearded Man, 4" ....$25.00 – 27.50

5th Row:
Father Cup and Saucer Set...$25.00 – 27.50 ea.

Page 122

Top Row:
"Horse and Cart"...$90.00 – 100.00

2nd Row:
"Singing Chicken" ....$40.00 – 50.00
"Sharp Shooter" ....$55.00 – 65.00

3rd Row:
"Circus Bear"...$90.00 – 100.00
"Kangaroo" ....$55.00 – 65.00
"Shimmy Donkey"...$45.00 – 50.00

4th Row:
"Lucky Sledge" ....$40.00 – 50.00
"Teddy's Cycle"..$50.00 – 60.00
"Fancy Dan, The Juggling Man" ....$75.00 – 85.00

Page 124

Top Row:
"Playful Little Dog"...$40.00 – 50.00
"Hurricane Racer"...$65.00 – 75.00
"Champion" ....$60.00 – 75.00

2nd Row:
"Singing Canary" ....$40.00 – 50.00
"Walking Bear"..$40.00 – 50.00
Penguin ....$30.00 – 40.00
"My Favorite Watch"..$8.00 – 10.00

3rd Row:
"Stem Winding Watch" ....$3.00 – 4.00 ea.
"Ice Cream Vendor" ....$75.00 – 85.00
Bamboo Snake, 15½"..$20.00 – 22.50
Rabbit...$18.00 – 20.00
"Hula" dancer (white) ....$50.00 – 60.00
"Hula" dancer (black) ....$75.00 – 85.00

4th Row:
"Ruby" Watch..$6.00 – 7.50
"Special" Cigar ....$8.00 – 10.00 ea.
Tool Set..$40.00 – 50.00
Dog..$18.00 – 20.00

Page 126

Top Row:
Brown, 4¼" ....$6.00 – 7.50
White, 4¾" ....$15.00 – 17.50
Swan, 5"...$10.00 – 12.50
Ballerina, 8¼" ....$50.00 – 60.00
Flowers in Relief, 10⅛" ....$50.00 – 60.00
Blue and White, 8¼" ....$12.50 – 15.00
Boy Ready for Picnic, 5".......................................$10.00 – 12.50

2nd Row:
Dragon in Relief, 2⅝" ....$8.00 – 10.00
Daffodil, 4" ....$6.00 – 7.50
Embossed Flower, 5½" ....$6.00 – 7.50
4th and 5th, 2¼" ....$4.00 – 5.00 ea.
Bisque, 4" ....$15.00 – 17.50
Bisque, 4" ....$15.00 – 17.50
Swan, 5" ....$10.00 – 12.50
9th and 10th 2⅝" and Bird in Relief, 4" ....$8.00 – 10.00 ea.
Dragon, 2½"...$4.00 – 5.00

3rd Row:
Tulip, 2⅜" ....$4.00 – 5.00
2nd and 9th, 3⅝" ....$5.00 – 6.00
Swan, 3¾" ....$10.00 – 12.50
"Wedgwood"-type, 6⅛" ....$40.00 – 50.00
Oriental Man, 4¾" ....$17.50 – 20.00
"Wedgwood"-type, 6⅝" ....$50.00 – 60.00
Scenic, 3¾" ....$12.50 – 15.00
Floral, 4¼" ....$6.00 – 7.50

4th Row:
2¼", "Pico" ....$4.00 – 5.00
2nd, 3rd, and 9th, 2¼" to 2½" ....$2.50 – 3.00 ea.
4th, 6th, 10th, 3" and 2" ....$4.00 – 5.00 ea.
5th, 3½", "Moriyama" ....$4.00 – 5.00
7th Elf, 2½" ....$7.00 – 8.50
8th Wall Pocket, 2½" ....$6.00 – 7.50
11th Floral, 3" ....$6.00 – 7.50
12th Seated Girl, 3½"..$10.00 – 12.50

5th Row:
1st "Wedgwood"-type, 2¾" ....$8.00 – 10.00
2nd and 11th, 3" and 2⅜".......................................$4.00 – 5.00
3rd Pagoda in Relief, 5¼" ....$20.00 – 22.50
4th, 7th, and 9th, 4½" to 4¾" ....$12.50 – 15.00
5th Tulip, 4" ....$10.00 – 12.50

6th Green, 4" ....$6.00 – 7.50
8th Cat Faces, 5" ....$20.00 – 22.50
10th Floral, 3" ....$5.00 – 6.00

Page 128

Top Row:
Frog, 4½" ....$15.00 – 17.50
Bowl, 7" ....$12.50 – 15.00
Plate, 8¼" ....$22.50 – 25.00
Horses, 7"..$30.00 – 35.00

2nd Row:
Flamingo Shakers...$12.50 – 15.00
3rd and 6th Cowgirl and Cowboy, 5½" ...$12.50 ea. or 25.00 – 27.50 pr.
Calves, 4¾"...$10.00 – 12.50 ea.
Dutch shakers, 3½" ....$12.50 – 15.00 pr.

3rd Row:
Tobies, 2¼" ....$15.00 ea. or 32.50 – 35.00 pr.
Bulldog, 4" ....$15.00 – 17.50
Cow Creamer, 8" ....$30.00 – 35.00
Swan, 2¾" ....$4.00 – 5.00
Vase, 2¾" ....$15.00 – 20.00

4th Row:
Celluloid Doll, 4½" ....$10.00 – 12.50
Doll, 2¾"...$6.00 – 7.50
Lady w/Flowers, 3½" ....$15.00 – 17.50
Wooden Coaster, set of eight, 2¾" ....$17.50 – 20.00
Metal Salt and Pepper Set ....$12.50 – 15.00
Tumbled Ice Skater ....$40.00 – 50.00

5th Row:
Doll, 5¼" ....$17.50 – 20.00
2nd thru 5th Plaques, 4¼" ....$6.00 ea. or 25.00 – 30.00 set

Page 130

Top Row:
1st and 4th Lamps, 12".................$70.00 ea. or 150.00 – 160.00 pr.
Lamp, 13"...$30.00 – 32.50
Lamp, 10"...$35.00 – 40.00

2nd Row:
1st and 3rd Bookends, 5¾" high ....$25.00 – 30.00 pr.
Basket, 10" ....$20.00 – 25.00

3rd Row:
Man, 8½"..$42.50 – 45.00
Man on Fence, 7½" ....$35.00 – 37.50
Couple, 7¾" x 8½"...$200.00 – 225.00
Sea Shell, 7" x 9" ....$85.00 – 100.00

Page 132

Wooden Box,14" x 22" $100.00
Jewelry Box, 12" x 5" ....$150.00 – 175.00
Record (set of 4)..$40.00 – 50.00

Page 134

Vase...$90.00 – 110.00

Page 6

Top Row:
Cherub, 5" ....$10.00 – 12.50
Cherub, 3⅝" ....$6.00 – 8.00
Angel w/Mandolin, 6⅜" ....$20.00 – 25.00
Cherub w/Horn, 6⅝" ....$25.00 – 30.00
Angel Pair, 6" ....$35.00 – 40.00

2nd Row:
1st, 3rd, 4th Angels ....$6.00 – 8.00 ea.
2nd, Cherub, pair ....$17.50 – 20.00
5th, Angel w/Lattice Basket...................$20.00 – 25.00

3rd Row:
Angel w/Mandolin, 2⅝" ....$4.00 – 5.00
Angel w/Drum ....$8.00 – 10.00
Cherub, pair w/grapes ....$20.00 – 25.00
4th, 5th, 6th, Angel Vases, 4" ....$10.00 – 12.00 ea.

4th Row:
1st – 7th, Angel Vases, 4" ....$10.00 – 12.00 ea.

5th Row:
1st – 4th, Angels, 2⅛" ....$5.00 – 6.00 ea.
5th – 7th, Angels, 3" ....$7.50 – 10.00 ea.
8th, Angel, 2½" ....$6.00 – 7.50

Page 8

Top Row:
Seated Dog, 4⅜" ....$20.00 – 25.00
"Luster," Dog ....$10.00 – 12.50
Gray and White Dog ....$12.50 – 15.00
Bird Dogs..$30.00 – 35.00
5th, Standing Dog, 7⅛" ....$17.50 – 20.00

2nd Row:
1st, 4th, 5th, and 8th, Dogs ....$15.00 – 17.50 ea.
2nd and 6th, Dogs ....$12.50 – 15.00 ea.
3rd, Collie ....$10.00 – 12.50
7th, Setter ....$12.50 – 15.00

3rd Row:
1st, 2nd, and 7th, Dogs.......................$7.50 – 10.00 ea.
3rd, Scottie ....$10.00 – 12.50
4th and 6th..$8.00 – 10.00 ea.
5th, Standing Dog ....$10.00 – 12.50

4th Row:
Standing ....$10.00 – 12.50
Scottie ....$12.50 – 15.00
Black and White.....................................$20.00 – 25.00
4th and 5th, Celluloid Scotties ....$6.00 – 8.00 ea.
Terrier ....$10.00 – 12.50
Scottie ....$12.50 – 15.00
Small ....$10.00 – 12.50

5th Row:
1st, 6th, and 7th, Groups ....$8.00 – 10.00 ea.

2nd, Big Ears..$6.00 – 8.00
3rd and 4th, Basket Dogs, 3" ....$10.00 – 12.50 ea.
5th, Scotties in Cart...............................$12.50 – 15.00

Page 10

Top Row:
Lion Pride, 4⅛" ....$45.00 – 50.00
Lion ....$5.00 – 6.00
Pig ....$8.00 – 10.00
4th, Seal..$6.00 – 8.00
5th, Squirrel..$10.00 – 12.50
6th, Squirrel, pair ....$30.00 – 35.00

2nd Row:
Green Elephant, 3¾" ....$15.00 – 17.50
Small Brown Elephant ....$7.50 – 10.00
Grayish-White Elephant, 4" ....$17.50 – 20.00
4th and 5th, Pink Elephants ....$4.00 – 5.00 ea.
Brown Elephants ....$10.00 – 12.50
Red Elephant ....$5.00 – 6.00
8th – 10th, Elephant Family Set...............$60.00 – 80.00
    Large ....$25.00 – 30.00
    Medium ....$20.00 – 25.00
    Small ....$15.00 – 20.00

3rd Row:
1st, 2nd, and 5th, Roosters ....$5.00 – 6.00 ea.
3rd, Large Rooster, 3½" ....$8.00 – 10.00
4th, Chicken Family..................................$20.00 – 25.00
6th, Butterfly ....$6.00 – 8.00

4th Row:
Monkey, missing piano, 3⅛" ....$8.00 – 10.00
    w/piano ....$12.50 – 15.00
2nd and 3rd, Monkeys w/Instruments.......$12.50 – 15.00
Monkey w/Horn ....$6.00 – 8.00
Monkey w/Dark Brown Suit ....$30.00 – 35.00
Three Monkey Set ....$10.00 – 12.00
Rabbit w/Drum ....$12.50 – 15.00
Rabbit w/Egg ....$6.00 – 8.00
Lobster ....$17.50 – 20.00

5th Row:
1st, 3rd, and 6th.....................................$6.00 – 8.00 ea.
Fish in Weeds ....$5.00 – 6.00
Clams, open or closed ....$5.00 – 6.00 ea.
Bisque Bass..$8.00 – 10.00
White Fish...$5.00 – 6.00

Page 12

Top Row:
1st – 4th, Swan Set..................................$90.00 – 120.00
    Small Swan ....$15.00 – 20.00 ea.
    Large Swan ....$40.00 – 50.00
    Swan Box ....$20.00 – 30.00

2nd Row:
Black Cigarette Box w/Floral Top.............$22.50 – 25.00

Cigarette Box w/Applied Roses.................................$20.00 – 22.50
Black Cigarette Box w/Floral Top...........................$22.50 – 25.00

3rd Row:
Ash Tray w/Bird ....$12.50 – 15.00
2nd – 4th, Ash Trays for above boxes ....$8.00 – 10.00 ea.
Fish Ash Tray...$7.50 – 10.00

4th Row:
Black Cigarette Box w/Orchid.................................$25.00 – 30.00
2nd Children Ash Trays ....$5.00 – 6.00 ea.
Pagoda Scene Box..$25.00 – 30.00
4th Children Ash Trays ....$5.00 – 6.00

5th Row:
House on Lake Scene Ash Tray...................................$7.50 – 10.00
Flower Cigarette Holder ....$17.50 – 20.00
Chamber Pot...$5.00 – 6.00
Swan w/Tail Cigarette Rest ....$6.00 – 8.00

Page 14
Top Row:
Embossed Rose Tray..$4.00 – 5.00
Floral Tray ....$2.50 – 4.00
Cigarette Holder...$4.00 – 5.00
Ash Tray, white w/blue..$10.00 – 12.50
Curled Leaf ....$2.50 – 4.00
"Wedgwood"-type Ash Tray ....$10.00 – 12.50

2nd Row:
Potty Seat ....$5.00 – 6.00
Same...$5.00 – 6.00
Hand..$4.00 – 5.00
Clown w/Heart ....$2.00 – 3.00
5th and 7th, Floral Trays ....$2.00 – 3.00 ea.
Teapot ....$2.50 – 4.00
Leaf ....$2.50 – 4.00

3rd Row:
1st and 2nd, Pig Bank Set ....$30.00 – 35.00
3rd and 6th, Pig Banks ....$25.00 – 35.00 ea.
4th, Pig Bank...$8.00 – 10.00
5th, Elephant Bank ....$25.00 – 35.00

4th Row:
1st – 3rd Baseball Players ....$17.50 – 20.00 ea.
Metal Fielder's Glove Ash Tray ....$12.50 – 15.00
5th and 7th, Bells ....$20.00 – 22.50 ea.
Dutch Girl Bell..$17.50 – 20.00

5th Row:
Owl Bird Cage Feeder ....$12.50 – 15.00
2nd and 3rd, Bookend..$35.00 – 40.00 pr.
4th and 5th, Dutch Bookend ....$35.00 – 40.00 pr.
Boxer...$12.50 – 15.00
Colonial Male Candle Holder ....$22.50 – 25.00

Page 16
Top Row:
Blue Buggy Planter, 5¼"..$8.00 – 10.00
2nd and 3rd, Buggies w/head on side ....$12.50 – 15.00 ea.
Same as 1st only pink...$8.00 – 10.00

2nd Row:
Reclining Clown ....$35.00 – 40.00
Clown Doing Hand Stand ....$35.00 – 40.00
Clown in Striped Suit, 5¼".......................................$40.00 – 50.00
Clown Playing Bass Fiddle ....$15.00 – 17.50
Clown, 5" ....$15.00 – 17.50
Reclining Clown ....$35.00 – 40.00

3rd Row:
1st – 3rd Cradles w/Child ....$12.50 – 15.00 ea.
Buggy w/bird on side ....$4.00 – 5.00
Small Buggy, 1⅞"..$5.00 – 6.00

4th Row:
Clown Playing Saxophone...$8.00 – 10.00
2nd – 4th, Clown w/Vase...$6.00 – 8.00 ea.
5th and 6th, Clown Salt and Pepper Set.....................$35.00 – 40.00 set

5th Row:
1st – 3rd Buggies in Brown, Pink, and Blue...............$12.50 – 15.00 ea.
4th, "Hummel-like" Girl w/Black Buggy ....$20.00 – 25.00

Page 18
Top Row:
Large Bird, 7⅞"...$30.00 – 35.00
Small Bird on Branch...$2.00 – 3.00
Pair of Birds ....$10.00 – 12.50
Pair of Birds ....$10.00 – 12.50
Large Bird on Planter, 7¾".......................................$30.00 – 35.00

2nd Row:
Colorful Bird...$12.50 – 15.00
Bird Bending ....$15.00 – 20.00
Bird on Branch ....$12.50 – 15.00
Small Birds on Branch ....$2.00 – 3.00
Blue Bird ....$4.00 – 5.00
Green Bird ....$6.00 – 8.00

3rd Row:
1st, 2nd, 3rd, and 5th, Stork or Pelican.....................$6.00 – 8.00 ea.
4th, Swan...$5.00 – 6.00
6th, Small Winged Bird ....$6.00 – 8.00
7th – 9th, Small Birds ....$4.00 – 5.00 ea.

4th Row:
Geese...$6.00 – 7.50 ea.

5th Row:
1st – 8th, Musical "Donald Ducks" ....$10.00 – 12.00 ea.
9th – 11th, Musical Long-Billed Ducks......................$6.00 – 8.00 ea.

Page 20
Top Row:
Bride and Groom, 6⅛"..$45.00 – 50.00
Lady w/Basket, 6½"..$25.00 – 30.00
Plaque, 6¼"...$25.00 – 30.00
Plaque, 6¾"...$35.00 – 40.00
Man Holding Hat, 6"..$25.00 – 30.00
Lady w/Dog and Gun...$25.00 – 30.00

2nd Row:
1st, Dancers, 3"...$10.00 – 12.50

2nd, Bride and Groom, 4¼" ....$20.00 – 25.00
3rd and 4th, Planter Pair, 5¼" ....$125.00 – 150.00 pr.
5th, Child Playing Accordion, 2¾" ....$10.00 – 12.50
6th, Boy w/Puppy ....$12.50 – 15.00

3rd Row:
1st, Man w/Umbrella, 3⅝" ....$12.50 – 15.00
2nd and 7th, Man and Woman ....$10.00 – 12.50 ea.
3rd, Lady, 5" ....$12.50 – 15.00
4th, Couple, 5⅝" ....$35.00 – 40.00
5th, Seated Couple w/Dog, 3⅝" ....$12.50 – 15.00
6th, Wall Pocket, 2⅜" ....$8.00 – 10.00
8th, Child w/Instrument ....$10.00 – 12.50

4th Row:
1st and 2nd, Planter Couple, 6¼" ....$30.00 – 40.00 pr.
3rd and 4th, Planters, 6" ....$60.00 – 75.00 ea.
5th, Fisherman, 7" ....$35.00 – 40.00
6th, Man w/Cape, 6" ....$20.00 – 25.00

Page 22

Top Row:
1st, Lady Planter, 6" ....$60.00 – 75.00
2nd and 3rd, Cart Planters, 7" ....$125.00 – 150.00 pr.
4th and 5th, Couple, 6½" ....$25.00 – 35.00 pr.

2nd Row:
1st and 2nd, Tree Vases, 4½" ....$17.50 – 20.00 pr.
3rd, Dancer..$6.00 – 8.00
4th and 5th, Musicians, 4½" ....$12.50 – 15.00 ea.
6th Drummer, 4½" ....$12.50 – 15.00
7th, Boy w/Rabbit ....$10.00 – 12.50
8th and 9th, Couple, 4¼" ....$17.50 – 20.00 pr

3rd Row:
1st and 2nd, Couple, 5⅜" ....$25.00 – 35.00 pr.
3rd, Kid Couple Planter ....$45.00 – 50.00
4th, Sunflower Kids ....$50.00 – 60.00
5th and 6th, Colonial Couple ....$30.00 – 35.00 pr.

4th Row:
1st and 2nd, Couple with Dogs, 7⅛" ....$90.00 – 100.00 pr.
3rd, Horse w/Rider, 10¼" ....$175.00 – 200.00
4th and 5th, Couple, 7¼" ....$75.00 – 85.00 pr.

Page 24

Top Row:
Football Players, 6" ....$12.00 – 15.00 ea.

2nd Row:
1st, Baby in Crocheted Dress....................$35.00 – 45.00
2nd – 4th, Rose Surprise ....$4.00 – 5.00 ea.
5th – 8th, Football Players, 4" ....$8.00 – 10.00 ea.
9th, Rickshaw ....$10.00 – 12.50

3rd Row:
Zoo Animals.......................................$8.00 – 10.00 ea.

4th Row:
Kewpie w/Feathers...............................$22.50 – 25.00
"Betty Boop," 8" ....$40.00 – 50.00
"Betty Boop," 6" ....$25.00 – 30.00

Baby, 11¾", moveable arms and legs ....$75.00 – 90.00
Dutch Girl, 8⅝" ....$40.00 – 50.00
Kewpie, 6½" ....$35.00 – 40.00

5th Row:
Black Hula Dancer w/Bows......................$35.00 – 40.00
Stork in Cage Window Bobber ....$17.50 – 20.00
Clown ....$17.50 – 20.00
Baby ....$12.50 – 15.00
Pink Snow Baby ....$15.00 – 17.50
Baby Rattle...$20.00 – 22.50

Page 26

Top Row:
Mallard Planter....................................$12.50 – 15.00
Duckling Near Hatched Egg Planter.............$10.00 – 12.00
Duckling in Egg Planter ....$10.00 – 12.00
2nd Row:
Rooster, Two-piece Covered Jar.................$35.00 – 40.00
Smaller Rooster Jar ....$25.00 – 30.00
Long-Billed Bird Planter..........................$5.00 – 6.00

3rd Row:
Goose Preening Planter ....$4.00 – 5.00
Chicken on Basket ....$30.00 – 35.00
Mallard Planter....................................$12.50 – 15.00

4th Row:
Small Duck Planter ....$4.00 – 5.00
Blue and Green Duck Planter ....$4.00 – 5.00
Duck w/Wings Raised............................$10.00 – 12.50

5th Row:
Goose Planter ....$4.00 – 5.00
Duck w/Egg Cart..................................$12.50 – 15.00
Blue and Green Duck ....$8.00 – 10.00
Chicken Pulling Cart ....$6.00 – 8.00

Page 28

Two Place Setting of 9 pieces ....$30.00 – 35.00
Four Place Setting of 13 pieces ....$50.00 – 55.00
Six Place Setting of 23 pieces ....$95.00 – 100.00
Six Place Setting of 26 pieces ....$115.00 – 125.00
*Add $5.00 to 10.00 for box in good condition.

Top Row:
1st, Blue Pottery-Like Creamer ....$6.00 – 8.00
2nd and 4th, Same Cup and Saucer ....$8.00 – 10.00
4th, Floral Luster Creamer.......................$8.00 – 10.00
5th, Same Sugar w/Lid...........................$10.00 – 12.50
6th, Doll's Nursing Set ....$50.00 – 60.00

2nd Row:
Camel Cup/Saucer ....$10.00 – 12.50
Miniature Eight Piece Set ....$8.00 – 10.00
Miniature Six Piece Set...........................$12.50 – 15.00
Miniature Ten Piece Set..........................$22.50 – 25.00
Blue Willow Gravy and Liner....................$50.00 – 55.00

3rd Row:
1st, Luster Sugar ....$6.00 – 8.00
2nd and 3rd, Creamers ....$6.00 – 8.00 ea.

4th, Yellow Floral Four-Piece Set ....$50.00 – 55.00

4th Row:
1st, Set, Orange Luster, Two Piece Set in Box ....$30.00 – 35.00
2nd, Set, Elephant Set Plate ....$10.00 – 12.00
Same Cup and Saucer ....$10.00 – 12.00
Same Sugar w/Lid.....................................$12.50 – 15.00
Same Teapot w/Lid....................................$17.50 – 20.00
Same Creamer...$10.00 – 12.00
3rd, Miniature Seven-Piece Set.......................$22.50 – 25.00

5th Row:
Seventeen-Piece Set in Box ....$90.00 – 100.00
Thirteen-Piece Set in Box ....$60.00 – 70.00

Page 30

Top Row:
Flower Girl, 4⅝" ....$12.50 – 15.00
Matching Bow w/Doll..................................$15.00 – 17.50
Boy w/Briefcase......................................$12.50 – 15.00
Matching Boy w/Book..................................$12.50 – 15.00
5th and 6th, Boy and Girl............................$25.00 – 30.00 pr.
7th and 8th, Girl w/Rabbit and Boy w/Dog ....$25.00 – 30.00 pr.

2nd Row:
1st and 2nd, Girl and Boy on Fence, 4" ....$30.00 – 35.00 pr.
3rd and 4th, Boy w/Horn and Girl w/Satchel ....$22.50 – 25.00 pr.
5th and 6th, Boy w/Toy Horse and Girl w/Doll.........$30.00 – 35.00 pr.
Boy w/Book ....$6.00 – 8.00
Boy w/Umbrella.......................................$6.00 – 8.00

3rd Row:
Girl w/Dog, 4⅛" ....$8.00 – 10.00
Girl w/Goose ....$6.00 – 8.00
Boy w/Duck and Basket................................$10.00 – 12.50
Boy w/Dog, 3" ....$6.00 – 8.00
Boy w/Dog, 4¼", Boy w/Rooster ....$10.00 – 12.50 ea.
Boy w/Walking Stick ....$8.00 – 10.00
Girl w/Umbrella and Dog ....$8.00 – 10.00

4th Row:
Girl w/"Betty Boop" doll, 3¾" ....$22.50 – 25.00
Girl w/Duck ....$4.00 – 5.00
Boy w/Bird Cage......................................$10.00 – 12.50
Boy on Fence w/Bird ....$5.00 – 6.00
Girl w/Basket ....$5.00 – 6.00
Girl on Fence..$5.00 – 6.00
"Little White Riding Hood," 4⅛" ....$12.50 – 15.00
Boy w/Horn...$5.00 – 6.00

5th Row:
Girl in Coat, 4⅛" ....$7.50 – 10.00
2nd and 3rd, Boys, 3¾"...............................$8.00 – 10.00 ea.
Girl w/Scarf...$5.00 – 6.00
Seated Girl w/Book...................................$5.00 – 6.00
Seated Girl w/Book...................................$6.00 – 8.00
Reclining Boy w/Horn.................................$7.50 – 10.00
Nude w/Wheat Sheaf ....$7.50 – 10.00

Page 32

Top Row:
Boy w/Saxophone, 4⅝" ....$6.00 – 8.00

Girl w/Teddy Bear, 5⅜"...............................$17.50 – 20.00
3rd and 4th, Goose Girls ....$10.00 – 12.50 ea.
Girl w/Lamb..$10.00 – 12.50
Boy w/Dog..$10.00 – 12.50
Boy on Fence ....$8.00 – 10.00
Blue Boy...$6.00 – 8.00

2nd Row:
1st – 4th, Skiers, 3½"...............................$12.50 – 15.00 ea.
5th and 6th, Skiers, 2⅛".............................$4.00 – 5.00 ea.
7th and 8th, Girl w/Flower or Book...................$4.00 – 5.00 ea.
9th, Boy on Fence w/Bird ....$5.00 – 6.00
10th, Boy w/Bike ....$7.50 – 10.00

3rd Row:
Girl w/Book/Basket, 3¾"..............................$5.00 – 6.00
Boy on Fence w/Basket, 4" ....$6.00 – 8.00
Boy w/Satchel ....$6.00 – 8.00
Same as 2nd except 3½"...............................$5.00 – 6.00
Boy w/Blue Bag.......................................$5.00 – 6.00
Boy Walker ....$5.00 – 6.00
Boy w/Dog ....$2.00 – 3.00
8th and 10th, Girl w/Book or Umbrella................$5.00 – 6.00 ea.
Dutch Boy ....$6.00 – 8.00

4th Row:
Girl w/Basket, 3⅛"...................................$4.00 – 5.00
2nd – 4th, Girl w/Duck and Boys w/Dog, 2¾" ....$2.50 – 4.00 ea.
Girl w/Doll ....$4.00 – 5.00
Girl w/Pitcher, 4" ....$6.00 – 8.00
Girl w/Curls ....$10.00 – 12.00
Girl w/Bucket ....$4.00 – 5.00
Boy w/Dog and Walking Stick ....$8.00 – 10.00
Walking Boy ....$10.00 – 12.50
Boy w/Dog, 2½".......................................$2.50 – 4.00

5th Row:
1st, Girl w/Doll Buggy, 2½"..........................$2.50 – 4.00
2nd, Boy w/Horn......................................$2.50 – 4.00 ea.
3rd, Girl w/Satchel ....$2.50 – 4.00 ea.
4th, Boy w/Truck ....$4.00 – 5.00
5th – 7th, Girls w/Book or Horn ....$4.00 – 5.00 ea.
8th, Girl w/Chick ....$5.00 – 6.00
9th, Boy w/Pig ....$5.00 – 6.00
10th and 11th, Boy w/Dog, Horn or on Fence...........$5.00 – 6.00 ea.
12th and 13th, Girls on Fence ....$5.00 – 6.00 ea.

Page 34

Top Row:
Set, pink w/flower...................................$20.00 – 22.00
Set, ...$8.00 – 10.00
Set ....$17.50 – 20.00

2nd Row:
Set ....$20.00 – 22.50
Set, yellow floral...................................$10.00 – 12.50
Set, black w/gold netting floral.....................$15.00 – 17.50

3rd Row:
Set, blue rim floral ....$8.00 – 10.00
Set, red rim floral ....$8.00 – 10.00
Set, w/emblem..$10.00 – 12.50

Set, w/house scene ....$10.00 – 12.50

4th Row:
Set, gold rimmed floral ....$8.00 – 10.00
Set, w/fancy M ....$8.00 – 10.00
Set, w/pagoda scene ....$10.00 – 12.50
Set, elephant head over A emblem ....$8.00 – 10.00

5th Row:
Set, blue w/floral.......................................$10.00 – 12.50
Set, LEDA in gold on side ....$15.00 – 17.50
Set, white floral ....$10.00 – 12.50
Set, floral w/fancy handle ....$12.50 – 15.00

Page 36

Top Row:
Set, black floral ....$17.50 – 20.00
Set, orange rim, floral ....$17.50 – 20.00
Set, black floral ....$17.50 – 20.00

2nd Row:
Set, blue and white ....$22.50 – 25.00
Set, floral..$10.00 – 12.50
Set, black floral ....$17.50 – 20.00

3rd Row:
Set, floral ....$8.00 – 10.00
Set, w/emblem..$10.00 – 12.50
Set, floral w/blue "luster" rim..................$8.00 – 10.00
Set, floral...$10.00 – 12.50

4th Row:
Set "Phoenix Bird".................................$22.50 – 25.00
Set, rust rimmed, floral ....$8.00 – 10.00
Set, floral w/stripe...................................$6.00 – 8.00
Set, floral w/blue "luster" rim.................$8.00 – 10.00

5th Row:
Set, tulip design..$10.00 – 12.50
Set, pink rimmed.......................................$8.00 – 10.00
Set, floral ribbed.......................................$15.00 – 17.50
Set, blue rimmed, floral interior................$10.00 – 12.50

Page 38

Top Row:
Set, floral demi ....$8.00 – 10.00
Set, white floral demi ....$8.00 – 10.00
Set, rose on tri-footed cup.........................$15.00 – 17.50
Set, white floral ....$8.00 – 10.00
Set, white floral ....$8.00 – 10.00

2nd Row:
Set, rust floral...$10.00 – 12.50

Set, blue floral rim....................................$8.00 – 10.00
Set, green floral rim ....$10.00 – 12.50
Set, footed, black w/gold ....$17.50 – 20.00

3rd Row:
Demi Set, black and white w/gold design..............$15.00 – 17.50
2nd – 5th, Sets, same as above only marked "No 6120
    Ardalt"...$15.00 – 17.50 ea.

4th Row:
Set, "Phoenix Bird," demi.........................$22.50 – 25.00
Set, yellow interior....................................$12.50 – 15.00
Set, white demi floral ....$6.00 – 8.00
4th and 5th, Sets, marked as in third row....................$12.50 – 15.00 ea.

5th Row:
Set, dark green swirl demi ....$22.50 – 25.00
Set, yellow demi..$10.00 – 12.50
Set (not Occupied Japan) ....$5.00 – 6.00
Set, "Royal Sealy" ....$12.50 – 15.00
Set, white floral swirled design..................$12.50 – 15.00

Page 40

Top Row:
Saucer, gray w/pink flower ....$2.00 – 3.00
Saucer, black w/pink flower ....$2.00 – 3.00
Saucer, black w/pink flower ....$2.00 – 3.00
Saucer, black acorn w/white oak leaf (?).......................$2.00 – 3.00

2nd Row:
Saucer, yellow rimmed ....$1.50 – 2.00
Saucer, blue w/pink flower ....$2.00 – 3.00
Saucer, yellow w/floral ....$2.00 – 3.00
Saucer, royal red w/flower ....$2.00 – 3.00

3rd Row:
Set, swirled white w/flower ....$6.00 – 8.00
Set, brown rim w/floral ....$5.00 – 6.00
Set, demi set floral ....$5.00 – 6.00
Set, demi "luster" w/floral ....$5.00 – 6.00
Set, demi six-sided black/red/white ....$10.00 – 12.50

4th Row:
Set, demi black floral ....$6.00 – 8.00
Sets, pagoda scene and green w/gold decoration ....$7.50 – 10.00 ea.
Set, white w/gold souvenir.........................$5.00 – 6.00
Set, pink floral ....$4.00 – 5.00
Set, blue w/scalloped rim ....$5.00 – 6.00

5th Row:
St. Denis, size 3", floral ....$10.00 – 12.50
St. Denis, size basket, decorated................$8.00 – 10.00
Set, "Mother," 4⅛" ....$25.00 – 30.00
Cup, "Mother," decorated floral ....$20.00 – 22.50

Page 42

Top Row:
Cuckoo Clock, 5"......................................$12.50 – 15.00
Christmas Bulb Tree ....$8.00 – 10.00
Christmas Bulbs...$25.00 – 30.00
Santas, red paper mache and blue w/silver hat ....$40.00 – 50.00 ea.

2nd Row:
Tree Ornaments..$10.00 – 12.50 ea.

3rd Row:
Clock, 2"..$6.00 – 8.00
2nd – 5th, Clocks, 3¾"..............................$8.00 – 10.00 ea.

4th Row:
1st, Child House..$4.00 – 5.00

37

2nd, 3rd, and 5th, Clocks ....$6.00 – 8.00 ea.
4th, Clock w/Dog..$8.00 – 10.00
6th, Cuckoo..$10.00 – 12.00

5th Row:
Coach, 3" high..$8.00 – 10.00
2nd and 3rd, Coaches, 2½" high ....$6.00 – 8.00 ea.
Occupied Japan Club Pin ....$15.00 – 17.50
Occupied Japan Collector's Club Mug ....$20.00 – 25.00

Page 44

Top Row:
Plate, 7"..$25.00 – 35.00
Plate, 6"..$20.00 – 25.00
Lattice Plate, 6"...$22.50 – 25.00
Fruit Plate..$20.00 – 22.50

2nd Row:
Candy or Relish, 5½" ....$6.00 – 8.00
Handled Plate, 4¼" ....$8.00 – 10.00
Handled Plate, 4¼" ....$8.00 – 10.00
4th and 5th, Floral Plates, 4½"........................$8.00 – 10.00 ea.

3rd Row:
1st – 3rd, Floral Bowls, 5½" ....$10.00 – 12.50 ea.
4th, Lattice-edge Floral Plate.............................$10.00 – 12.50
5th, Lattice-edge Fruit Bowl, 5½" ....$15.00 – 17.50

4th Row:
Brown Tri-Plate ....$10.00 – 12.50
Brown Leaf-Shaped Plate ....$8.00 – 10.00
Brown Floral Plate, Brown Bowl........................$4.00 – 5.00 ea.
Brown Cloverleaf Shape Plate ....$8.00 – 10.00

Page 46

Top Row:
1st and 5th, Small Leaf, 2½".............................$2.00 – 3.00 ea.
2nd – 4th, Fruit Plates, 6" ....$12.50 – 15.00 ea.

2nd Row:
Palette, signed "V. Soga".................................$12.50 – 15.00
Palette, signed "K. Ohi"...................................$10.00 – 12.50
Oval, 7½" Latticed-edged Bowl ....$20.00 – 22.50
Bowl, 4½", lattice edge ....$12.50 – 15.00

3rd Row:
1st, Maple Leaf ....$2.00 – 3.00
2nd, Dog Plate, 2¾"..$8.00 – 10.00
3rd and 5th, Small Flower Plate.......................$2.00 – 3.00 ea.
4th, Leaf w/Bee ....$4.00 – 5.00
6th, Tray w/Translation..$8.00 – 10.00
7th, Embossed Rose on Tray ....$4.00 – 5.00

4th Row:
1st, Fish on Shell-Shaped Tray ....$8.00 – 10.00
2nd and 5th, Scenic Plates ....$2.50 – 4.00 ea.
3rd and 4th, Scenic Plates ....$4.00 – 5.00 ea.
6th, Clover Scene..$8.00 – 10.00
7th, Sea Shell, 3"..$2.50 – 4.00

5th Row:
Handled Floral Bowl...$12.50 – 15.00

Sea Shell, 4"..$4.00 – 5.00
Handled "Luster" Bowl...$7.50 – 10.00
Handled Plate, 4¼" ....$6.00 – 8.00
Handled Plate, 4¼" ....$6.00 – 8.00

Page 48

Set for 4...$175.00 – 200.00
Set for 6...$225.00 – 250.00
Set for 8...$275.00 – 300.00
Set for 12...$400.00 – 450.00

Page 54

Top Row:
Cereal Bowl, 5¾"...$12.50 – 15.00
Sugar w/Lid...$17.50 – 20.00
Creamer...$12.50 – 15.00
Berry Bowl, 4¾" ....$10.00 – 12.50

2nd Row:
Cup and Saucer ....$17.50 – 20.00
Salad Plate, 7"...$6.00 – 8.00
Dinner Plate, 9"...$12.50 – 15.00

3rd Row:
Demitasse Cup and Saucer...................................$20.00 – 22.00
Cup and Saucer ....$15.00 – 17.50
Demitasse Saucer ....$4.00 – 5.00
Cup and Saucer ....$17.50 – 20.00
Ash Tray...$4.00 – 5.00
Bowl, berry, 4" to 4⅞" ....$5.00 – 6.00
Bowl, cereal, 5" to 6½" ....$6.00 – 8.00
Bowl, soup, 7" to 9"..$10.00 – 12.00
Bow, round vegetable, 9½" to 10½"....................$25.00 – 35.00
Bowl, oval vegetable, 10" to 12" ....$30.00 – 40.00
Casserole, covered ....$45.00 – 65.00
Comport or Compote ....$20.00 – 22.50
Creamer...$12.50 – 15.00
Cup ....$8.00 – 15.00
Gravy...$12.50 – 15.00
Gravy Platter ....$8.00 – 10.00
Gravy w/Attached Platter....................................$25.00 – 30.00
Plate, bread and butter 5¾" to 6¾" ....$2.50 – 4.00
Plate, salad, 7" to 8"...$5.00 – 6.00
Plate, dinner, 9" to 11"...$15.00 – 20.00
Platter, small oval, 9½" to 11" ....$15.00 – 20.00
Platter, medium oval, 12" to 15" ....$25.00 – 35.00
Platter, large turkey, 16" to 19" ....$50.00 – 85.00
Saucer..$1.00 – 3.00
Sugar w/Cover ....$15.00 – 20.00

Page 56

Top Row:
1st and 2nd, Aborigine Pair, 4¾"......................$40.00 – 50.00
Snake Charmer Couple Vase, 5½".....................$20.00 – 22.50
Black Fiddling Boy..$20.00 – 22.50
Indian Winding Turban, 6"..................................$17.50 – 20.00
"Mammy" Pie Bird ....$125.00 – 150.00

2nd Row:
Boy w/Fiddle, 3" ....$15.00 – 17.50
Boy w/Horn, 3" ....$15.00 – 17.50
Gray Faced Fiddler ....$12.50 – 15.00

Cowboy on Horse .... $10.00 – 12.50
Cowboy Vase .... $10.00 – 12.50
Indian Girl Bud Vase, 3⅝" .... $8.00 – 10.00
Indian Chief Bud Vase, 3⅝" .... $8.00 – 10.00

3rd Row:
1st and 2nd, Dutch Pair .... $17.50 – 20.00 ea.
Hula Girl w/Grass Skirt .... $7.50 – 10.00
Hula Girl .... $10.00 – 12.50
Indian Head Metal Pencil Sharpener .... $15.00 – 20.00
Ash Tray, metal, "Howdy Podner" .... $4.00 – 5.00
Indian Head .... $12.50 – 15.00

4th Row:
Dutch Girl, 3¼" .... $5.00 – 6.00
Dutch Girl Shaker .... $6.00 – 8.00
Dutch Boy Bust Shaker .... $6.00 – 8.00
Dutch Boy w/Pipe .... $5.00 – 6.00
Dutch Girl w/Basket, 4½" .... $12.50 – 15.00
Dutch Girl w/Basket, 3⅛" .... $8.00 – 10.00
Dutch Girl Seated Shaker .... $6.00 – 8.00
Dutch Boy w/Buckets .... $8.00 – 10.00

5th Row:
Girl with Bowl on Head 4½" .... $6.00 – 8.00
Girl w/Bowl on Head and Vase, 5" .... $7.50 – 10.00
Cowboy, 5⅛" .... $8.00 – 10.00
4th and 5th, Dutch Couple, 6⅛" .... $17.50 – 20.00 ea.
6th and 7th, Snake Charming .... $25.00 – 30.00 pr.

Page 59

Top Row:
Couple, 7¼" .... $40.00 – 50.00
Couple, 6½" .... $100.00 – 125.00
Couple, 7½" .... $35.00 – 50.00

2nd Row:
Couple, 5" .... $22.50 – 25.00
Couple w/Dogs, 5½" .... $25.00 – 30.00
Couple w/Arms Up and Dogs .... $40.00 – 45.00
Dutch People at Well .... $25.00 – 30.00

3rd Row:
Colonial Couple, 10⅛" .... $75.00 – 100.00
Couple, 10" .... $60.00 – 75.00

4th Row:
Couple w/Hats, 6½" .... $40.00 – 50.00
Couple .... $75.00 – 100.00
Couple, 6½" .... $30.00 – 40.00

Page 60

Top Row:
Couple, 6⅛" .... $30.00 – 40.00
Couple, 6" .... $50.00 – 60.00
Couple, 7" .... $30.00 – 35.00
Couple, 5¼" .... $25.00 – 30.00

2nd Row:
Couple, 5¼" .... $35.00 – 45.00
Couple, 4⅝" .... $15.00 – 20.00
Couple .... $15.00 – 20.00
Dutch Couple, 4⅛" .... $15.00 – 20.00
Colonial Couple .... $10.00 – 12.00
Couple in White .... $8.00 – 10.00

3rd Row:
Couple, 7½" .... $40.00 – 50.00
Colonial Couple, 7¼" .... $50.00 – 60.00
Couple, 8⅛" .... $75.00 – 90.00
Couple, 7" .... $35.00 – 45.00

4th Row:
Couple, 6⅛" .... $35.00 – 40.00
Hatted Couple .... $20.00 – 25.00
Musical Couple .... $40.00 – 50.00
Couple, 6⅜" .... $35.00 – 40.00

Page 61

Top Row:
Colonial Couple, 5⅝" .... $25.00 – 30.00
Colonial Couple, 8¹⁄₁₆" .... $55.00 – 70.00
Couple, 7" .... $50.00 – 60.00

2nd Row:
Couple, 4⅛" .... $15.00 – 20.00
Couple w/Flowers .... $15.00 – 20.00
Couple in Fancy Dress .... $15.00 – 20.00
Blue Couple .... $20.00 – 25.00

3rd Row:
1st and 2nd Couples, 5" .... $15.00 – 20.00 pr.
Couple .... $15.00 – 20.00
Colonial Couple .... $20.00 – 25.00

4th Row:
Pastel Couple, 5" .... $15.00 – 20.00
Couple .... $15.00 – 17.50
Couple .... $15.00 – 17.50
Couple, 4" .... $10.00 – 12.00

5th Row:
Musical Couple, 4⅝" .... $20.00 – 25.00
Seated Musicians, 4⅛" .... $20.00 – 25.00
Same as 2nd only 3½" .... $12.50 – 15.00
Seated, 3" .... $25.00 – 30.00

Page 63

Top Row:
Couple, 4" .... $10.00 – 12.50
Couple, 4⅞" .... $12.50 – 15.00
Couple, 5⅜" .... $17.50 – 20.00
Bisque Set, 4⅝" .... $10.00 – 12.50 ea.

2nd Row:
Seated Pair, 2¾" .... $20.00 – 25.00
2nd and 3rd, Old and Young .... $12.50 – 15.00 pr.
Couple, 3⅛" .... $7.50 – 10.00
Boy and Girl, 4⅝" .... $12.50 – 15.00

3rd Row:
Couple, 8¼" .... $30.00 – 40.00
Dancers, 7½" .... $75.00 – 100.00
Couple, 7" .... $30.00 – 40.00

4th Row:

1st – 5th, Set, 7½" ....$17.50 – 20.00 ea.

6th – 9th, Set ....$15.00 – 17.50 ea.

Page 64

Top Row:

1st and 3rd, Couple, 6½" ....$20.00 – 25.00 pr.

2nd, Couple, 4" ....$8.00 – 10.00

4th, Couple w/Pig ....$20.00 – 25.00

5th, Couple, 4" ....$12.50 – 15.00

2nd Row:

1st, Kissing Couple ....$30.00 – 32.50

2nd and 3rd same as 1st only marked in red.............$30.00 – 32.50 pr.

3rd Row:

1st and 2nd, Couples, 8¼" ....$60.00 – 75.00 pr.

3rd, Skinny Yellow Couple, 7¼" ....$22.50 – 25.00

4th Row:

Similar to Page 63, Row 3 ....$30.00 – 40.00

Older Couple ....$30.00 – 35.00

Children, 7½" ....$40.00 – 50.00

Couple, 6⅛" ....$25.00 – 30.00

Page 65

Top Row:

1st, Singing Boy, 5½" ....$10.00 – 12.50

2nd, Man w/Hat ....$12.50 – 15.00

3rd and 5th Lady and Man ....$10.00 – 12.50 ea.

4th, Warrior on Horse, 6½" ....$22.50 – 25.00

6th, Lady ....$6.00 – 8.00

7th, Boy w/Basket ....$12.50 – 15.00

2nd Row:

1st, Warrior, 3¾" ....$6.00 – 8.00

2nd, Bearded Man ....$7.50 – 10.00

3rd and 7th – 9th, Musicians ....$10.00 – 12.50 ea.

4th and 5th, Boys ....$6.00 – 8.00 ea.

6th, Lady w/Child ....$20.00 – 22.00

3rd Row:

1st, Girl, 5¾", w/Folded Hands ....$8.00 – 10.00

2nd and 5th, Man w/Beard or Flute ....$10.00 – 12.50 ea.

3rd, Girl with Basket, 8" ....$20.00 – 25.00

4th and 7th, Man and Woman..............................$12.50 – 15.00 ea.

6th, Musician w/Foot Up, 6¼" ....$12.50 – 15.00

8th, Seated Boy ....$6.00 – 8.00

4th Row:

1st, Warrior, 4⅛" ....$7.50 – 10.00

2nd and 3rd, Girl or Boy ....$8.00 – 10.00 ea.

4th, Rickshaw ....$15.00 – 17.50

5th, Oriental Cowboy ....$15.00 – 17.50

6th, Couple ....$7.50 – 10.00

7th, Boy, 7⅞" ....$20.00 – 22.50

8th, Dancer..$15.00 – 20.00

Page 67

Top Row:

1st, Lady w/Basket, 5¾" ....$8.00 – 10.00

2nd and 6th, Lady w/Fan or Basket ....$10.00 – 12.50 ea.

3rd, Lady w/Purple Skirt.....................................$12.50 – 15.00

4th, Brown/White Lady, 8¼" ....$30.00 – 40.00

5th, Lady Lifting Skirt ....$17.50 – 20.00

7th, Peasant Lady ....$12.50 – 15.00

2nd Row:

1st, Lady w/Mandolin, 4" ....$5.00 – 6.00

2nd, 4th, and 5th, Ladies ....$10.00 – 12.00 ea.

3rd, Gent, 3¾" ....$2.50 – 4.00

6th, 8th, and 9th, Ladies ....$4.00 – 5.00 ea.

7th, Lady w/Basket, 5⅜" ....$10.00 – 12.50

10th, Lady, K.I. in emblem ....$4.00 – 5.00

3rd Row:

1st, Lady w/Red Shawl, 3½" ....$4.00 – 5.00

2nd – 4th, Ladies w/Dog or Deer, 4½" ....$15.00 – 17.50 ea.

5th and 8th, Ladies, 5" ....$12.50 – 15.00 ea.

6th and 7th, Ladies ....$6.00 – 8.00 ea.

4th Row:

1st and 6th, Ladies, 7⅛" ....$15.00 – 17.50 ea.

2nd, Well Endowed Lady, 8" ....$30.00 – 35.00

3rd, Lady w/Feathers in Hair, 10⅜"....................$75.00 – 90.00

4th, Buxom Lady, 10" ....$75.00 – 90.00

5th, Peasant Lady, 8" ....$25.00 – 30.00

Page 68

Top Row:

1st, Seated Man, 4½" ....$10.00 – 12.50

2nd and 5th, Seated Ladies, 5⅛" ....$12.50 – 15.00 ea.

3rd and 4th, Lady Planters, 6⅜" ....$15.00 – 17.50 ea.

6th, Couple on Bench..$8.00 – 10.00

7th, Couple on Couch, 4" ....$17.50 – 20.00

2nd Row:

1st, 2nd, and 6th, Seated, 3" ....$5.00 – 6.00 ea.

3rd, Children on Couch ....$20.00 – 25.00

4th, Seated Lady ....$4.00 – 5.00

5th, Seated Man ....$10.00 – 12.50

7th, 9th, and 10th, Seated Figures, 2¾" ....$2.50 – 4.00 ea.

8th, Seated Couple ....$17.50 – 20.00

3rd Row:

1st and 2nd, Couple, 3" ....$10.00 – 12.50 pr.

3rd and 4th, Couple ....$6.00 – 8.00 pr.

5th and 6th, Couple ....$10.00 – 12.50 pr.

7th – 9th, Ladies ....$7.50 – 10.00 ea.

4th Row:

1st, Lady w/Living Bra, 4½"...............................$5.00 – 6.00

2nd – 4th, Men ....$2.50 – 4.00 ea.

5th, Lady w/Dog ....$15.00 – 17.50

6th, 8th, and 9th, Ladies ....$6.00 – 8.00 ea.

7th, Lady ....$8.00 – 10.00

5th Row:

1st, Lady, 4" ....$6.00 – 8.00

2nd, 3rd, 9th – 11th, Figures ....$6.00 – 8.00 ea.

4th Lady ....$2.50 – 4.00

5th and 6th, Seated Ladies ....$4.00 – 5.00 ea.

7th Man ....$2.50 – 4.00

8th Lady ....$7.50 – 10.00

Page 69

Top Row:
1st, Man w/Blue Coat, 6" ....$10.00 – 12.50
2nd, 4th, and 5th, Men ....$10.00 – 12.50 ea.
3rd, Man w/Emblem in Red..................$12.50 – 15.00
6th, Mandolin Player..................$17.50 – 20.00
7th and 8th, Men ....$10.00 – 12.50 ea.

2nd Row:
1st, Balloon Man, 3½" ....$12.50 – 15.00
2nd and 3rd, Men ....$6.00 – 8.00 ea.
4th – 8th, Men ....$4.00 – 5.00 ea.
9th and 10th, Men ....$7.50 – 10.00 ea.

3rd Row:
1st – 3rd, Men, 4⅛" ....$4.00 – 5.00 ea.
4th – 6th Men ....$2.50 – 4.00 ea.
7th and 8th, Men ....$6.00 – 8.00 ea.
9th and 10th, Men ....$7.50 – 10.00 ea.
11th, Man Holding Flower..................$10.00 – 12.50

4th Row:
1st, Man w/Violin, 8⅛" ....$40.00 – 50.00
2nd, Man w/Tricorn Hat, 9⅝" ....$50.00 – 60.00
3rd and 4th, Mandolin Players, 10⅛" ....$60.00 – 75.00 ea.
5th, Man w/Blue Coat and Tricorn Hat, 10⅝" ....$85.00 – 100.00
6th, Swashbuckler, 10" ....$60.00 – 75.00

Page 70

Top Row:
Lady Holding Dress, 4¼" ....$10.00 – 12.50
Lady Holding Hat, 5" ....$12.50 – 15.00
Lady Holding Skirt ....$15.00 – 17.50
Lady in Curtsy..................$12.50 – 15.00

2nd Row:
Ballerina, 3⅝" ....$17.50 – 20.00
Ballerina, green dress..................$20.00 – 25.00
Ballerina, 4¼" and Ballerina, 3½" ....$20.00 – 25.00

3rd Row:
1st, Dancer, blue dress, 4"..................$6.00 – 8.00
2nd, Dancer, yellow dress, 3½"..................$5.00 – 6.00
3rd and 5th, Dancers, 2½"..................$2.50 – 4.00 ea.
4th, Dancer, 3"..................$4.00 – 5.00
6th, Dancer w/Leg Exposed, 4"..................$6.00 – 8.00

4th Row:
Dancer, orange dress, 3¼" ....$5.00 – 6.00
Dancer, 2½" ....$2.50 – 4.00
Dancer ....$2.00 – 3.00
4th – 7th, Dancers ....$2.50 – 4.00 ea.

5th Row:
Ballerina, 5¾" ....$30.00 – 40.00
Wind-swept Lady, 6½" ....$20.00 – 25.00
Lady Holding Dress, 6¼" ....$20.00 – 25.00
Ballerina w/Turquoise Skirt, 6¼" ....$30.00 – 40.00

Page 72

Top Row:
1st and 2nd, Elephant Sets ....$25.00 – 35.00 ea.

3rd and 5th, Blue Atomizers ....$25.00 – 30.00 ea.
4th, Blue Perfume ....$20.00 – 25.00
6th, Icon, 5⅛" ....$30.00 – 40.00

2nd Row:
1st, 2nd, and 5th, Perfumes w/Dauber, 3½" ....$20.00 – 25.00 ea.
3rd, Crystal Perfume w/Dauber ....$17.50 – 20.00
4th, Salt Shaker, 2⅜" ....$10.00 – 12.50
6th, Blue Goose..................$6.00 – 8.00

3rd Row:
Incense Burner, 4¼"..................$17.50 – 20.00
Same except 4"..................$17.50 – 20.00
Same as 1st except crown emblem ....$17.50 – 20.00
Black Incense Burner..................$30.00 – 40.00
White Elephant Incense Burner ....$17.50 – 20.00

4th Row:
1st, Incense Burner, 4¼"..................$17.50 20.00
2nd, Dragon Incense Burner $12.50 15.00
3rd and 4th, Mexican Incense Burners ....$25.00 – 30.00 ea.
5th, Elephant Incense Burner..................$25.00 – 35.00

5th Row:
Modern Inkwell..................$12.50 – 15.00
China Inkwell..................$75.00 – 100.00

Page 74

Top Row:
Strand of pearls, ...$10.00 – 12.50 ea.
    Package of 10..................$50.00 – 60.00
"Butterfly Brooch," card of 24..................$30.00 – 40.00
Strand of Pearls ....$12.50 – 15.00
Strand of Miniature Beads ....$15.00 – 17.50

2nd Row:
Rhinestone Bracelet ....$30.00 – 50.00
Rhinestone Bracelet ....$30.00 – 50.00
Crossed Swords Pin ....$12.50 – 15.00
4th – 8th, Celluloid Pins ....$8.00 – 10.00 ea.

3rd Row:
Scottie Dog in Sweater..................$12.50 – 15.00
Dog Head ....$10.00 – 12.50
3rd – 5th, Celluloid Bird Pins ....$10.00 – 12.50 ea.

4th Row:
1st, Two Dog Head Pin ....$10.00 – 12.50
2nd-4th, Celluloid Brooch and Earring Set..................$25.00 – 30.00
5th, Shamrock ....$2.50 – 4.00
6th, Two Dog Head Pin ....$10.00 – 12.50

Page 76

Top Row:
Ice Bucket, 7⅝"..................$50.00 – 60.00
Vase w/Leaf Design, 13" ....$125.00 – 150.00
Plate w/Pagoda Scene ....$30.00 – 40.00

2nd Row:
Black Box, 5½" x 9" ....$50.00 – 65.00
Five Leaf Clover Tray..................$40.00 – 50.00
Red Box ....$50.00 – 65.00

3rd Row:
1st, Candy Tray w/Metal Handle ....$20.00 – 25.00
2nd, Cup w/Rattan Handle ....$15.00 – 17.50
3rd, Piano ....$40.00 – 50.00
4th and 5th, Vases ....$30.00 – 40.00 ea.
6th, Basket ....$50.00 – 65.00

Page 78

Top Row:
1st and 3rd, Colonial Pair ....$75.00 – 90.00
2nd, Lamp, 8⅜" ....$35.00 – 40.00

2nd Row:
1st and 2nd, Colonial Couple, 7⅛" ....$65.00 – 75.00 pr.
3rd, Colonial Couple, 7⅝" x 5⅛" ....$27.50 – 35.00
4th, Lamp, same as 3rd except 7½" x 5" ....$25.00 – 32.50

3rd Row:
Colonial Couple Seated...$25.00 – 35.00
Man with Urn...$30.00 – 40.00
Colonial Pair ....$27.50 – 35.00

Page 80

Top Row:
Lorelei Bud Vase ....$8.00 – 10.00
Lorelei Planter ....$12.50 – 15.00
Lorelei w/Cello ....$8.00 – 10.00
Lorelei Bud Vase ....$8.00 – 10.00
5th – 7th, Lorelei ....$8.00 – 10.00 ea.

2nd Row:
Orange-tail Mermaid on Rocks..................................$20.00 – 25.00
Blue-tail Mermaid on Rocks.....................................$20.00 – 25.00
Same as 2nd only unpainted ....$17.50 – 20.00
Bisque, 3½", orange tail..$20.00 – 22.50
5th and 6th, Lorelei Bud Vases.................................$8.00 – 10.00 ea.

3rd Row:
1st and 2nd, Same as 4th in second row ....$20.00 – 25.00 ea
3rd, Mermaid Holding Blue Tail ....$20.00 – 25.00
4th, Mermaid Sitting w/Orange Tail...........................$20.00 – 25.00
5th, Mermaid w/Small Blue-tipped Tail ....$20.00 – 22.50
6th and 7th, Reclining Mermaids, 4⅜" ....$25.00 – 30.00 ea.

4th Row:
1st and 3rd, Fish Bowl Pagodas ....$10.00 – 12.50 ea.
2nd and 4th, Mermaid Sitters...................................$17.50 – 20.00 ea.
5th, Mermaid on Shell..$20.00 – 25.00
6th, Pagoda..$6.00 – 8.00

5th Row:
1st, 4th, and 5th, Fish Bowl Pagodas ....$10.00 – 12.50 ea.
2nd and 3rd, Fish Bowl Pagodas................................$10.00 – 12.50 ea.

Page 82

Top Row:
Buddha Tray...$10.00 – 12.00
New York City Souvenir Tray ....$5.00 – 6.00
Ornate Serving Tray...$12.50 – 15.00

2nd Row:
1st, Louisiana Souvenir Tray ....$4.00 – 5.00

2nd, New York Heart w/Statue of Liberty.................$10.00 – 12.50
3rd, 5th and 6th, Ash Trays....................................$2.00 – 3.00 ea.
4th, Ash Tray ....$2.50 – 4.00

3rd Row:
Candy, three part..$10.00 – 12.50
Florida Souvenir Tray ....$4.00 – 5.00
Chicago Souvenir Tray ....$4.00 – 5.00
Ornate Gold-colored Ash Tray ....$4.00 – 5.00
Ornate Silver-plated Ash Tray ....$5.00 – 6.00

4th Row:
Oval Tray ....$5.00 – 6.00
Ash Tray w/Peacock ....$2.50 – 4.00
Six-piece Cigarette Set..$20.00 – 25.00
Yellowstone Park Souvenir Tray ....$4.00 – 5.00

5th Row:
Colorado Souvenir Tray...$4.00 – 5.00
Howe Cabins NY ....$4.00 – 5.00
Ornate Blue Ash Tray ....$4.00 – 5.00
Six-piece Miniature Tea Set.......................................$20.00 – 25.00
El Paso, c. 1950..$5.00 – 6.00

Page 84

Top Row:
Ash Tray...$20.00 – 22.50
Celluloid Piano...$20.00 – 25.00
Metal Piano...$17.50 – 20.00
"Photolite" Table Lighter...$25.00 – 35.00
Gold Ball Lighter ....$15.00 – 18.00

2nd Row:
Knight Lighter..$10.00 – 15.00
Knight Lighter..$10.00 – 15.00
Camel Lighter ....$15.00 – 20.00
Elephant Lighter..$15.00 – 20.00
Rocket Ship Lighter..$25.00 – 30.00
Scottie Dog Lighter..$15.00 – 17.50

3rd Row:
Fish Lighter...$12.50 – 15.00
Desk Lighter..$5.00 – 6.00
Normal-style Lighter...$4.00 – 5.00
Aladdin-type Lighter...$6.00 – 8.00
Lighter...$5.00 – 6.00
Desk Lighter..$6.00 – 8.00

4th Row:
Peacock Lighter ....$10.00 – 12.50
Fancy Dragon Six-piece Cigarette Set.........................$25.00 – 35.00
Floor Model Radio Lighter ....$20.00 – 25.00
Barrel "Chicago"...$10.00 – 12.50

5th Row:
1st – 3rd, Horse Head Lighters ....$12.50 – 15.00 ea.
Boot Lighter with Ash Tray ....$8.00 – 10.00
Two Boots w/Hat Ash Tray ....$15.00 – 17.50 set

Page 86

Top Row:
Basket..$17.50 – 20.00

Floral Vase ....$12.50 – 15.00
Urn Vase ....$10.00 – 12.50
Copper Urn Vase w/Grapes ....$12.50 – 15.00
Container w/Lid ....$12.50 – 15.00

2nd Row:
Bird Cage Clock..............................$225.00 – 250.00
Bowl w/Three Angel Feet....................$12.50 – 15.00
3rd and 4th, Sugar/Creamer Set ....$20.00 – 22.50

3rd Row:
Red Ring Box ....$10.00 – 12.50
Dragon Cigarette Box and Tray.................$12.50 – 15.00
Box ....$10.00 – 12.50

4th Row:
Inkwell w/Pen Holder ....$15.00 – 20.00
Bowl, 4-footed w/lid ....$12.50 – 15.00
Heart Box ....$10.00 – 12.50
Box w/Peacock ....$15.00 – 17.50

5th Row:
Candy Compote ....$10.00 – 12.50
Cowboy Hat and Glove Top ....$8.00 – 10.00
Lockable Box ....$12.50 – 15.00
Small Box w/Peacock ....$8.00 – 10.00

Page 88

Top Row:
Creamer..$8.00 – 10.00
Corn Sugar w/Lid................................$12.50 – 15.00
Corn Creamer......................................$8.00 – 10.00
Corn Marmalade ....$12.50 – 15.00
Flower Basket Cookie Jar ....$20.00 – 25.00

2nd Row:
Rice Bowl..$6.00 – 8.00
Tea Cup ....$6.00 – 8.00
Corn Marmalade ....$15.00 – 17.50
Tea Cup, bird scene..............................$7.50 – 10.00
Rice Bowl, floral.................................$5.00 – 6.00
Orange Marmalade ....$12.50 – 15.00

3rd Row:
Pink Lily of Valley Sugar ....$10.00 – 12.50
Soup Spoon ....$10.00 – 12.50
Corn Container.....................................$4.00 – 5.00
Fruit Basket...$20.00 – 22.50
Basket Weave Butter Dish ....$17.50 – 20.00
Egg Cup ....$6.00 – 8.00

4th Row:
1st, Saki Cup in front ....$5.00 – 6.00
2nd, Ship Rice Bowl ....$6.00 – 8.00
3rd, 5th, 7th and 9th, Saki Cups.............$5.00 – 6.00 ea.
4th Dragon Rice Bowl ....$7.50 – 10.00
6th, Large Rice Bowl ....$8.00 – 10.00
8th, Red Floral Rice Bowl ....$7.50 – 10.00
10th, Large Rice Bowl ....$8.00 – 10.00

5th Row:
Iris Small Creamer ....$10.00 – 12.50

Small 4-footed Floral Oval Bowl...................$5.00 – 6.00
Saki Cup...$4.00 – 5.00
Lobster Sugar w/Lid ....$30.00 – 35.00
Lobster Creamer...................................$15.00 – 20.00
Lobster 3-part Tray ....$30.00 – 40.00

Page 91

Top Row:
Cowboy Mug ....$25.00 – 30.00
Cowboy Mug ....$20.00 – 22.50
Santa Mug ....$30.00 – 35.00
Brown Elephant Mug, 4¾" ....$17.50 – 20.00

2nd Row:
People Mugs..$20.00 – 22.50 ea.

3rd Row:
Nickel-plated 5" Mugs ....$35.00 – 50.00 ea.

4th Row:
1st, Indian Head Mug............................$10.00 – 12.50
2nd, Small Mug ....$5.00 – 6.00
3rd, Small Mug ....$5.00 – 6.00
4th, Cupids w/Bow ....$10.00 – 12.50

Page 92

Large Umbrella, 22" before open ....$25.00 – 35.00 ea.
Open Umbrella.....................................$12.50 – 15.00
"Transfer Picture" Books, intact ....$30.00 – 50.00 ea.
Floral Fans ....$12.00 – 20.00 ea.
Large Black Fan ....$20.00 – 25.00
Small Black Fan ....$12.50 – 15.00

Page 93

Top Row:
1st, Leaves ....$2.50 – 4.00
2nd and 4th, Party Favors, 6" ....$5.00 – 6.00 ea.
3rd, 4th etc., Party Horns ....$5.00 – 6.00 ea.

2nd Row:
1st, "Spot The Spot" Puzzle ....$6.00 – 8.00
2nd – 8th, Noise Makers ....$2.50 – 4.00 ea.
9th and 10th, Paper Drink Umbrellas ....$1.00 – 1.50 ea.

3rd Row:
"Old Glory" Bow Tie............................$5.00 – 6.00
Pin Box ....$7.50 – 10.00
Celluloid Basket Tape Measure ....$20.00 – 25.00
4th and 5th, Needle Packs ....$8.00 – 10.00 ea.
6th and 7th, Celluloid Pig Tape Measure....$20.00 – 25.00 ea.
8th and 9th, Colonial Couple Pin Cushions ....$8.00 – 10.00 ea.

4th Row:
1st Cat Pin Cushion ....$5.00 – 6.00
2nd, Dog Pin Cushion ....$5.00 – 6.00
3rd and 4th, Half-doll Pin Cushions ....$30.00 – 35.00 ea.
5th – 8th, Colonial Pin Cushions ....$8.00 – 10.00 ea.

5th Row:
1st – 5th, Cat and Dog Pin Cushions ....$6.00 – 8.00 ea.
6th, Oriental Lady Pin Cushion, 6" ....$12.50 – 15.00

43

Page 95

Top Row:

1st, Parrot ....$15.00 – 17.50

2nd and 3rd, Hanging Bird Planters w/24" chain ....$35.00 – 50.00 ea.

4th, Bird Planter ....$7.50 – 10.00

2nd Row:

Elephant Planters ....$12.50 – 15.00 ea.

3rd Row:

1st, White Elephant Planter.......................................$5.00 – 6.00

2nd and 4th, Rearing Elephants ....$8.00 – 10.00 ea.

3rd, Brown Elephant ....$15.00 – 18.00

5th and 6th, Smaller versions of second row ....$7.50 – 10.00 ea.

4th Row:

1st and 2nd, Birds on Fence and Cow............................$6.00 – 8.00 ea.

3rd and 4th, Pig or Frog ....$15.00 – 18.00 ea.

5th Row:

1st – 3rd, Elephant or Bird Planters............................$8.00 – 10.00 ea.

4th, Bear on Blue Tree ....$10.00 – 12.50

5th, Blue Squirrel ....$8.00 – 10.00

Page 96

Large Donkey...$10.00 – 12.50 ea.

Medium Donkeys...$6.00 – 8.00 ea.

Smaller Donkeys...$3.00 – 5.00 ea.

Page 97

Top Row:

1st and 2nd, Lambs ....$6.00 – 8.00 ea.

3rd, Hanging Parrot..$35.00 – 45.00

4th, Parrot ....$15.00 – 18.00

5th, Hanging Parrot w/24" chain................................$50.00 – 65.00

2nd Row:

1st – 3rd, Lambs...$12.50 – 15.00 set

4th, Lamb ....$2.50 – 4.00

5th, Pink Bunny ....$10.00 – 12.50

6th and 7th, Bunnies ....$10.00 – 12.50 ea.

3rd Row:

1st, Woodpecker Eyeing Frog.....................................$4.00 – 5.00

2nd – 4th, Birds ....$6.00 – 8.00 ea.

5th, Green Donkey ....$6.00 – 8.00

4th Row:

1st, Medium Donkey...$6.00 – 8.00

2nd – 8th, except 6th...$3.00 – 5.00 ea.

6th, Donkey ....$4.00 – 5.00

5th Row:

1st, Zebra...$6.00 – 8.00

2nd, Dog Cart...$5.00 – 6.00

3rd, Very Small Donkey Cart ....$2.00 – 3.00

4th and 5th, Cow Carts...$7.50 – 10.00 ea.

6th, Cow Planter...$6.00 – 8.00

Page 98

Top Row:

1st and 2nd, Oriental Girl and Boy, 4⅛" ....$7.50 – 10.00 ea.

3rd, Head Planter ....$10.00 – 12.50

4th and 5th, Oriental Boy and Girl, 5" ....$12.50 – 15.00 ea.

6th, Big Hat Oriental, 5⅛" ....$6.00 – 8.00

7th, Shelf Sitter Planter ....$12.50 – 15.00

2nd Row:

1st, Seated Mandolin Player ....$6.00 – 8.00

2nd and 3rd, Boy w/Rickshaw ....$10.00 – 12.50 ea.

4th, Oriental Couple..$15.00 – 17.50

5th, Carriage Boy ....$4.00 – 5.00

3rd Row:

Heart w/Angel, 3⅝" ....$10.00 – 12.00

Umbrella Girl ....$6.00 – 8.00

Chicken Feeding Boy...$6.00 – 8.00

Girl Reading Book ....$8.00 – 10.00

Girl w/Accordion ....$4.00 – 5.00

Colonial Man, 4⅝" ....$10.00 – 12.50

4th Row:

1st and 2nd, Dutch Boy and Girl, 4½" ....$15.00 – 18.00 ea.

3rd, Girl matches 6th in row above............................$10.00 – 12.50

4th, Couple ....$4.00 – 5.00

5th, Girl w/Urn ....$5.00 – 6.00

6th, Boy playing Ukulele ....$8.00 – 10.00

5th Row:

1st and 2nd, Boy and Girl on Fence w/Dog, 4¾" ....$8.00 – 10.00 ea.

3rd, Dutch Girl w/Buckets ....$8.00 – 10.00

4th, Girl w/Duck, 4⅝" ....$6.00 – 8.00

5th, Sleepy Mexican...$8.00 – 10.00

Page 100

Top Row:

Oriental Vase ....$12.50 – 15.00

Oriental Girl...$15.00 – 17.50

"Hummel-type" Angel ....$50.00 – 60.00

Peacock Wall Pocket..$20.00 – 22.50

Flamingo Wall Plaque..$25.00 – 30.00

2nd Row:

1st, Wooden Ship ....$12.50 – 15.00

2nd and 3rd, Small Flattened Cornucopias ....$4.00 – 5.00 ea.

4th, Iris Wall Pocket ....$12.50 – 15.00

5th, Rose on Black Wall Plaque ....$12.50 – 15.00

6th, Parrot Wall Pocket ....$35.00 – 40.00

7th, Cup and Saucer Holder ....$2.50 – 4.00

3rd Row:

Wooden Cigarette Box Bird Retriever.........................$30.00 – 40.00

Wooden Cigarette Box..$20.00 – 25.00

Wooden Rickshaw ....$12.50 – 15.00

Bamboo Handled Tray...$20.00 – 22.50

4th Row:

Wooden Spoon..$8.00 – 10.00

Magic Trick Box ....$20.00 – 22.50

Dog House with Dog ....$8.00 – 10.00

Decorative Straw Basket...$35.00 – 45.00

5th Row:

1st, Apple Wall Plaque ....$8.00 – 10.00

2nd and 4th, Mallard Plaques....................................$15.00 – 17.50 ea.
3rd, Pipe Cleaner Man ....$12.50 – 15.00
5th, Green Horse Plaque ....$20.00 – 22.50
6th, Dutch Boy ....$20.00 – 22.50

Page 102

Top Row:
1st, Cobalt Blue Shakers, Mustard with Spoon on Tray ....$45.00 – 50.00
2nd, Urns w/Tray ....$20.00 – 22.50
3rd, Cobalt Blue Set....................................$45.00 – 50.00

2nd Row:
Coffee Pot Set ....$12.50 – 15.00
Skillet, flowers on tray....................................$20.00 – 22.50
Urns on Tray ....$15.00 – 17.50
Teapots on Tray ....$15.00 – 17.50
Penguins....................................$20.00 – 22.50

3rd Row:
Tall Gold Colored Shakers....................................$15.00 – 17.50
Box and Shakers to its right....................................$20.00 – 22.50 set

4th Row:
Cocktail Shakers on Tray....................................$20.00 – 22.50
Single Elephant....................................$12.50 – 15.00
Single Urn ....$5.00 – 6.00
Souvenir Shakers ....$12.50 – 15.00
Candles on Tray ....$20.00 – 22.50
Single Coffee Pot....................................$6.00 – 8.00

5th Row:
Cowboy Boots....................................$12.50 – 15.00
Egg set; cup and shakers....................................$20.00 – 25.00
Lamp Set....................................$15.00 – 20.00
Ship ....$22.50 – 25.00
Single Donkey Piled w/Tools ....$10.00 – 12.50

Page 104

Top Row:
1st, Strawberry Salt and Pepper on Tray ....$20.00 – 25.00
2nd and 4th, Strawberry Shakers, 3⅝"....................................$17.50 – 20.00
3rd, Strawberry Covered Sugar....................................$15.00 – 17.50
4th, Windmill Teapot....................................$40.00 – 50.00

2nd Row:
Windmill Small Creamer, 2⅝" ....$8.00 – 10.00
Windmill Sugar w/Lid, 3⅞"....................................$17.50 – 20.00
Windmill Teapot, 4⅞" ....$35.00 – 40.00
Windmill Large Creamer, 2⅞" ....$8.00 – 10.00
Salt and Pepper Set, w/teapot....................................$15.00 – 20.00

Third Row
Set, salt, pepper and mustard on tray ....$30.00 – 35.00
Covered Dish ....$25.00 – 30.00
Butter Dish....................................$35.00 – 40.00
4th – 7th, Butter Pats....................................$10.00 – 12.50 ea.

4th Row:
Teapot ....$50.00 – 65.00
Cookie or Biscuit Jar....................................$90.00 – 100.00
Sugar and Creamer on Tray ....$30.00 – 35.00

Page 106

Top Row:
Bisque Fisherman, 5"....................................$17.50 – 20.00
Bisque Fisherman....................................$12.50 – 15.00
Bisque Fisherman....................................$12.50 – 15.00
Book Reader....................................$25.00 – 30.00
5th and 6th, Oriental pair. ....$12.50 ea. or 27.50 – 30.00 pr.

2nd Row:
1st, Girl w/Red Hat ....$17.50 – 20.00
2nd, Boy Holding Hat....................................$12.50 – 15.00
3rd and 4th, Colonial Couple ....$8.50 ea. or 17.50 – 20.00 pr.
5th, Dutch Girl ....$12.50 – 15.00
6th, Dutch Boy....................................$12.50 – 15.00
7th, Girl w/Song Book ....$12.50 – 15.00

3rd Row:
Boy w/Horn, 3¾" ....$10.00 – 12.50
Oriental Boy....................................$12.50 – 15.00
Girl w/Ruffles ....$17.50 – 20.00
Girl w/Doll, 5" ....$20.00 – 22.50
Bisque Couple....................................$10.00 – 12.50
Girl w/Flowers ....$10.00 – 12.50
Boy Playing Banjo ....$8.00 – 10.00

4th Row:
Ballerina, 6⅛" ....$35.00 – 40.00
Boy....................................$10.00 – 12.50
Oriental Playing Mandolin....................................$10.00 – 12.50
Oriental Playing Mandolin....................................$8.00 – 10.00
Oriental ....$8.00 – 10.00
Blue Boy ....$8.00 – 10.00

5th Row:
Girl in Green Dress, 3⅝" ....$8.00 – 10.00
Girl w/Instrument....................................$10.00 – 12.50
Girl w/Music Book ....$15.00 – 17.50
Oriental w/Musical Instrument....................................$10.00 – 12.50
Bisque Cowgirl ....$12.50 – 15.00

Page 108

Top Row:
1st, Pitcher w/Yellow Flower, 3⅛"....................................$2.50 – 4.00
2nd and 4th, Pitchers w/Brown Design....................................$2.00 – 3.00 ea.
3rd, Floral Pitcher ....$4.00 – 5.00
5th, Pitcher, 5⅛" ....$6.00 – 8.00
6th, Green Pitcher w/Orange Flower ....$4.00 – 5.00
7th, Blue Pitcher w/Draped Lady....................................$6.00 – 8.00
8th, Pitcher w/Basket Weave Design....................................$2.50 – 4.00

2nd Row:
1st, Ornate Water Can, 3" ....$10.00 – 12.00
2nd, White Can w/Raised Pink Rose ....$5.00 – 6.00
3rd and 4th, White w/Red Rose or Basket Weave....................................$4.00 – 5.00 ea.
5th, Floral Can ....$2.00 – 3.00
6th, Yellow Can w/Raised Rose ....$5.00 – 7.00
7th, Blue Can w/Raised Pink Rose ....$5.00 – 8.00

3rd Row:
1st and 12th, Coffee Pots, 2"....................................$4.00 – 5.00 ea.
2nd – 6th, 10th, Pitchers ....$2.50 – 4.00 ea.
7th – 9th, Water Cans....................................$2.00 – 3.00 ea.

11th, Pitcher ....$2.50 – 4.00

4th Row:
1st, Pitcher, 2⅜" ....$2.50 – 4.00
2nd, Ornate Handle Pitcher................................$5.00 – 6.00
3rd, Small Pitcher, 1¾" ....$2.50 – 4.00
4th, White Pitcher w/White Raised Rose.................$2.50 – 4.00
5th and 6th, Matching Urns, 3⅛"........................$2.50 – 4.00 ea.
7th, White Pitcher w/Pink Rose ....$2.00 – 3.00
8th and 9th, Pitchers w/Raised Roses ....$5.00 – 6.00 ea.
10th, Bird Pitcher ....$10.00 – 12.50

5th Row:
Water Can, 1¾" ....$1.00 – 1.50
White Floral Pitcher.......................................$2.50 – 4.00
Blue Pitcher...$2.50 – 4.00
Pitcher ....$2.50 – 4.00
White Teapot w/Lid ....$5.00 – 6.00
Coffee w/Raised Flower and Lid ....$10.00 – 12.00
Same only teapot..$6.00 – 8.00
Round Teakettle w/Lid ....$5.00 – 6.00
Coffee Pot w/Lid...$6.00 – 8.00

Page 110

Top Row:
Demitasse Set...$125.00 – 150.00
Cup and Saucer ....$10.00 – 12.50 ea.
Teapot ....$60.00 – 75.00

2nd Row:
Gray Teapot ....$25.00 – 30.00
Demitasse Cup and Saucer..................................$8.00 – 10.00
Rust w/Floral Teapot......................................$20.00 – 25.00

3rd Row:
Demitasse Set...$155.00 – 180.00
Cup and Saucer ....$10.00 – 12.50 ea.
Creamer...$12.50 – 15.00
Sugar w/Lid...$17.50 – 20.00
Teapot ....$60.00 – 70.00

4th Row:
Brown Glaze Individual Teapot.............................$10.00 – 12.50
Brown Glazed Teapot w/Floral Design ....$20.00 – 22.50
Individual Brown Glaze Teapot w/Lid ....$6.00 – 8.00

Page 112

Top Row:
1st, Luster Ware Floral Demitasse Set.....................$10.00 – 12.50
2nd, Tea Set for Six ....$75.00 – 100.00
Creamer...$8.00 – 10.00
Sugar w/Lid...$10.00 – 12.50
Teapot ....$25.00 – 30.00
Cup and Saucer (not pictured) ....$6.00 – 7.00

2nd Row:
Pink Floral Set for Six...................................$200.00 – 250.00
Creamer...$10.00 – 12.50
Sugar w/Lid...$17.50 – 20.00
Teapot ....$60.00 – 70.00
Cup and Saucer ....$12.50 – 15.00
Plate...$8.00 – 10.00

3rd Row:
Floral w/Ivy Set for Four ....$100.00 – 125.00
Creamer...$8.00 – 10.00
Sugar w/Lid...$12.50 – 15.00
Teapot ....$35.00 – 40.00
Cup and Saucer ....$10.00 – 12.00

4th Row:
Demitasse Set...$8.00 – 10.00
Sugar w/Lid...$10.00 – 12.50
Red Bird Teapot...$35.00 – 40.00
Demitasse Cup/Saucer......................................$8.00 – 9.00
Set for Six w/Stand.......................................$50.00 – 60.00
Individual Teapot...$12.50 – 15.00

Page 114

Top Row:
"Hopping Dog" ....$20.00 – 25.00
"Cowboy w/Two Guns".......................................$60.00 – 75.00
Celluloid "Toddling Babe" ....$50.00 – 60.00

2nd Row:
"Playing Dog" ....$50.00 – 60.00
"Monkey Sweet Melodian"...................................$75.00 – 90.00
Celluloid Swan on Box ....$22.50 – 25.00
"Auto Cycle"..$300.00 – 400.00

3rd Row:
"Sparkling Loop Plane" ....$150.00 – 200.00
"Penguin"...$30.00 – 40.00
"Remote Control Car"......................................$100.00 – 125.00

4th Row:
"Camel"...$80.00 – 100.00
Small Car ....$20.00 – 25.00
Celluloid "Cheery Cook" ....$60.00 – 75.00
Celluloid Boy "Circus Tricycle"...........................$75.00 – 100.00

5th Row:
1st, Inflatable Football ....$20.00 – 22.50
2nd and 3rd, Inflatable Rabbits...........................$15.00 – 17.50 ea.

Page 116

Top Row:
Monkey on Tricycle..$75.00 – 100.00
Monkey ....$50.00 – 75.00
Celluloid Baseball Catcher ....$75.00 – 100.00
Metal Dog ....$40.00 – 50.00
Celluloid Clown Monkey....................................$65.00 – 80.00
Celluloid Xylophone Player................................$100.00 – 125.00

2nd Row:
Celluloid Rabbit..$100.00 – 125.00
Walking Camel ....$45.00 – 55.00
Walking Metal Duck..$25.00 – 30.00
Flipping Celluloid Clown ....$60.00 – 75.00

3rd Row:
Metal Tricycle, missing rider.............................$15.00 – 17.50
Celluloid Boy w/Metal Case................................$60.00 – 75.00
Wind-up Car, 5" ....$50.00 – 60.00
Celluloid Flipping Monkey.................................$50.00 – 65.00

Wind-up Car, 3" ....$25.00 – 30.00

4th Row:
Hopping "Rudolph" Reindeer.....................$60.00 – 75.00
Celluloid Walking Santa ....$400.00 – 450.00
Roller Skating Bear.............................$200.00 – 225.00
Walking, Hopping Giraffe ....$50.00 – 60.00
Celluloid Acrobatic Gymnast ....$125.00 – 130.00

5th Row:
Walking Lion ....$40.00 – 50.00
Hopping Dog w/Bone ....$40.00 – 50.00
Walking Elephant...............................$40.00 – 50.00
Walking Dog ....$30.00 – 35.00

Page 118

Top Row:
"Angora Rabbit," three colors..................$25.00 – 30.00 ea.

2nd Row:
Hopping Squirrel...............................$100.00 – 120.00
"Jumping Rabbit"...............................$25.00 – 30.00

3rd Row:
1st and 2nd, "Studebaker" ....$60.00 – 75.00 ea.
3rd, "Baby Pontiac" ....$40.00 – 45.00
4th, "Chevrolet with Back Motion" ....$60.00 – 75.00

4th Row:
"Sarcus" Celluloid Elephant ....$300.00 – 350.00
"Circus Elephant" ....$275.00 – 325.00
"Sarcus" Celluloid Monkey ....$300.00 – 350.00

5th Row:
Celluloid "Cowboy".............................$75.00 – 90.00
"Trick Seal" w/Celluloid Ball ....$50.00 – 65.00
Celluloid Pink Seal ....$50.00 – 65.00

Page 120

Top Row:
Vase w/Floral Decoration, 8"...................$40.00 – 45.00
Same as 1st, except 6".........................$30.00 – 35.00
Cornucopia.....................................$12.50 – 15.00
Pottery Vase...................................$17.50 – 20.00
Raised Rose Bud Vase ....$12.00 – 15.00
Cylinder Vase, 8"..............................$25.00 – 35.00

2nd Row:
1st, Floral Two-handled, 4⅞" ....$6.00 – 8.00
2nd, Rust Floral...............................$8.00 – 10.00
3rd and 4th, Cornucopias w/Floral Design ......$6.00 – 8.00 ea.
5th, Two-handled Floral........................$5.00 – 6.00
6th, Pottery Decorated ....$15.00 – 17.50
7th, Orange Floral ....$6.00 – 7.50
8th, Blue Floral ....$8.00 – 10.00

3rd Row:
1st, Floral, 2⅝"...............................$2.00 – 3.00
2nd, Tulip.....................................$2.00 – 3.00
3rd, Blue Open Handled ....$2.50 – 4.00
4th – 8th, Mini Vases ....$2.00 – 3.00 ea.
9th, Windmill Design ....$4.00 – 5.00

10th, Floral ....$2.00 – 3.00
11th, Spatter Ware ....$6.00 – 8.00
12th, Embossed Children, 3" ....$10.00 – 12.00

4th Row:
Green Floral, 3⅞"..............................$7.50 – 10.00
Blue w/Pink Flower ....$6.00 – 8.00
Orange Flower ....$7.50 – 10.00
Footed Vase ....$5.00 – 6.00
Mexican Siesta ....$10.00 – 12.50
6th – 9th, Brown Vases ....$4.00 – 5.00 ea.

5th Row:
1st – 7th, Brown Vases, 3¾" to 4" ....$6.00 – 8.00 ea.
8th and 9th, Brown Vases ....$4.00 – 5.00 ea.

Page 122

Top Row:
Girl w/Apron, 4⅞" ....$10.00 – 12.50
Same, only 3⅞".................................$8.00 – 10.00
Chinese Boy in Vase, 6⅛".......................$30.00 – 35.00
Colonial Lady in Vase ....$30.00 – 35.00
Two-handled Child ....$20.00 – 25.00
Colonial Man, 3¼"..............................$5.00 – 6.00
Child w/Basket.................................$7.50 – 10.00

2nd Row:
Oriental Lad, 4½"..............................$12.50 – 15.00
Oriental Lady ....$20.00 – 25.00
Cowboy w/Cactus ....$12.50 – 15.00
Boy w/Accordion ....$5.00 – 6.00
"Hummel"-type Boy w/Violin ....$15.00 – 17.50
Girl ....$8.00 – 10.00

3rd Row:
Colonial Girl, 2½".............................$2.50 – 4.00
Clown w/Egg ....$12.50 – 15.00
Brown Vase....................................$4.00 – 5.00
Boy w/Cart ....$5.00 – 6.00
Colonial by Flower ....$5.00 – 6.00
Mexican by Cactus ....$5.00 – 6.00
7th and 8th, Colonials ....$4.00 – 5.00 ea.

4th Row:
1st and 2nd, Colonial Lady or Man, 3½" ....$6.00 – 8.00 ea.
3rd, Vase w/Dancer.............................$8.00 – 10.00
4th, Child ....$4.00 – 5.00
5th, Lady w/Blue Basket........................$4.00 – 5.00
6th, Pottery-like Vase.........................$5.00 – 6.00
7th – 9th, Lady or Man, 2" ....$2.50 – 4.00 ea.

5th Row:
1st, Brown Vase, 2½" ....$5.00 – 6.00
2nd, Orange Vase, 2½" ....$5.00 – 6.00
3rd – 6th, Oriental Vases, 2½".................$5.00 – 6.00 ea.
7th, Oriental ....$7.50 – 10.00
8th and 9th, Oriental, 2½".....................$5.00 – 6.00 ea.

Page 125

Top Row:
1st and 2nd, Oriental Couple, 10½".............$100.00 – 125.00 pr.
3rd, Bamboo Mat ....$20.00 – 25.00

Bottom Row:
Needle Point..$200.00 – 250.00
Musketeer, 17¼"......................................$200.00 – 300.00

Page 126
Clock..$300.00 – 350.00

Page 127

Left foreground; Bird Cage Clock...........................$225.00 – 250.00

Left background; Musician Couple, 10⅛".............$125.00 – 150.00 pr.
Center foreground; China Inkwell.............................$75.00 – 90.00
Center; Tea Set...$75.00 – 100.00
Teapot..$40.00 – 50.00
Creamer...$15.00 – 17.50
Sugar w/Lid...$20.00 – 25.00
Center background; Musketeer, 17¼"....................$200.00 – 300.00
Right foreground; Souvenir China Casserole.............$75.00 – 85.00
Right background; Cinderella and
    Prince Charming, 8¼"...$100.00 – 125.00

Page 6

Top Row:
1st, Cherub, 5¾" ....$25.00 – 30.00
2nd and 5th, Cherubs ....$30.00 – 35.00 ea.
3rd and 4th, Angels Playing Tambourine, 7¼"............$60.00 – 75.00 ea.

2nd Row:
Angel on Pink Basket, 5" ....$50.00 – 55.00
Angel with Shell on Back, 5⅛"..............................$40.00 – 45.00
Angel Sitting on Cornucopia ....$55.00 – 65.00
Angel w/Donkey, 4⅛" ....$25.00 – 30.00

3rd Row:
Cherub Holding Bowl, 5½" ....$45.00 – 55.00
Angel Fixing Halo..$45.00 – 50.00
Angel at Anvil...$45.00 – 50.00
Angel w/Donkey ....$50.00 – 60.00

4th Row:
Cherub Vase, 3⅜"...$12.50 – 15.00
Angel w/Shell ....$35.00 – 40.00
Angel w/Wheelbarrow ....$25.00 – 30.00
4th and 5th Angel Bud Vases, 5¼" ....$17.50 – 20.00 ea.

5th Row:
1st, Angel Planter..$30.00 – 35.00
2nd and 4th, Angels on Butterfly..........................$20.00 – 25.00 ea.
3rd, Powder Box ....$75.00 – 90.00
5th, Angel w/Shell ....$25.00 – 30.00

Page 8

Top Row:
Plume-tail Peacock, 5" ....$17.50 – 20.00
Flamingo ....$20.00 – 22.50
Bird ....$2.50 – 4.00
Blue Birds ....$7.50 – 10.00
Small Birds on Limb..$2.00 – 3.00
Bird w/Long Tail...$4.00 – 5.00
Penguin ....$6.00 – 7.00
Fancy Plume-tailed Peacock.................................$17.50 – 20.00

2nd Row:
1st and 2nd, Birds on Limb...................................$2.00 – 3.00 ea.
3rd, Duck w/Hat..$6.00 – 8.00
4th and 6th, Birds on Limb ....$7.50 – 10.00 ea.
5th, Bird on Limb..$7.50 – 10.00
7th, Birds on Stump ....$8.00 – 10.00

3rd Row:
1st and 3rd, Chick ....$2.00 – 3.00 ea.
2nd, Swan...$2.50 – 4.00
4th and 8th – 11th, Birds......................................$2.50 – 4.00 ea.
5th – 7th, Birds ....$2.50 – 4.00 ea.

4th Row:
Frog w/Accordion ....$10.00 – 12.50
Frog w/Bass Fiddle ....$10.00 – 12.50
Frog on Lily Pad ....$17.50 – 20.00
Frog Drummer ....$17.50 – 20.00

Frog w/Accordion ....$17.50 – 20.00
6th and 7th, Frog w/Violin or Mandolin.....................$15.00 – 17.50 ea.

5th Row:
Bear w/Hat ....$8.00 – 10.00
Hugging Pandas ....$10.00 – 12.50
Brown Bear ....$10.00 – 12.50
Polar Bear (?) ....$5.00 – 6.00
Frog Ash Tray ....$10.00 – 12.50
Frog Vase ....$12.50 – 15.00
Bisque Frog Fish Bowl Ornament ....$12.50 – 15.00
Reclining Frog ....$15.00 – 17.50

Page 10

Top Row:
Cat Planter, 3⅝"..$6.00 – 8.00
Cat Sitting ....$20.00 – 22.50
Cat Reclining ....$20.00 – 22.50
Cat Planter...$5.00 – 6.00
Cat w/Bow ....$6.00 – 8.00

2nd Row:
Cat w/Pert Expression..$2.50 – 4.00
Cat w/Kitten ....$2.50 – 4.00
Black Cat w/Basket..$5.00 – 6.00
Cat w/Bee-like Tail ....$2.50 – 4.00
Cat w/Bow ....$4.00 – 5.00
Cat w/Paw Up ....$4.00 – 5.00
Cat w/Tail Up...$5.00 – 6.00
Cat w/Tiger Tail..$2.50 – 4.00
Black Cat..$5.00 – 6.00

3rd Row:
1st, Curly Tail Cat...$2.50 – 4.00
2nd – 4th, Set w/Ball, Yarn, Bug...........................$2.00 – 3.00 ea.
5th and 7th, Cats in Potty.....................................$2.00 – 3.00 ea.
6th, Cat w/Red Yarn ....$5.00 – 6.00
8th, Bull Dog with Rubber Tail ....$7.50 – 10.00
9th, Dog Sitting ....$5.00 – 6.00
10th, Dog Walking ....$2.50 – 4.00

4th Row:
1st and 2nd, Yellow and Blue Dog Planters, 4"..............$4.00 – 5.00 ea.
3rd and 4th, Long Dogs ....$6.00 – 8.00
5th, Dog w/Hat and Pipe, 3½" ....$10.00 – 12.50
6th, Dog, same except 2⅜" ....$5.00 – 6.00

5th Row:
1st and 2nd, Brown or Black Dog Planters....................$5.00 – 6.00 ea.
3rd, Dog Sitting ....$8.00 – 10.00
4th, Spotted Dog Planter ....$5.00 – 6.00
5th and 6th, Dog Planters.....................................$5.00 – 6.00 ea.

Page 12

Top Row:
1st, Pony..$6.00 – 8.00
2nd, Jumping Horses 5" ....$35.00 – 45.00
3rd and 4th, Horses ....$12.50 – 15.00 ea.
5th, Donkey..$6.00 – 8.00

6th, Deer..$2.50 – 4.00

2nd Row:
Metal Horse w/Saddle...$10.00 – 12.50
Metal Donkey w/Prospecting Gear...........................$10.00 – 12.50
Saddle Horse w/Cork ....$10.00 – 12.50
Deer...$6.00 – 8.00
Cow ....$8.00 – 10.00
Goat ....$6.00 – 8.00

3rd Row:
1st, Lady Bug w/Bat, 2¼"..$6.00 – 8.00
2nd and 3rd, Lady Bug w/Hat or Umbrella ....$5.00 – 6.00 ea.
4th, Lady Bug w/Newspaper...$5.00 – 6.00
5th, Lady Bug w/Bass Fiddle and Top Hat, 3" ....$6.00 – 8.00
6th, Lady Bug w/Mandolin and Polka Dot Hat ....$6.00 – 8.00
7th, Lady Bug w/Horn and Turban ....$6.00 – 8.00
8th, Lady Bug w/Violin ....$6.00 – 8.00
9th, Lady Bug w/Bag ....$5.00 – 6.00
10th, Lady Bug w/Accordion..$6.00 – 8.00

4th Row:
1st, Lady Bug w/Vest 3½"...$7.50 – 10.00
2nd, Lady Bug Ice Man ....$10.00 – 12.50
3rd, Lady Bug w/Lantern..$10.00 – 12.50
4th and 5th, Lady Bug w/Soda and Singer ....$7.50 – 10.00 ea.
6th, Lady Bug w/Buggy...$6.00 – 8.00
7th, Lady Bug w/Camera ....$10.00 – 12.50

5th Row:
Lady Bug w/Bat, 4" ....$12.50 – 15.00
Lady Bug w/Broom..$10.00 – 12.50
Lady Bug w/Umbrella..$10.00 – 12.50
Lady Bug Indian w/Pipe ....$12.50 – 15.00
Same marked...$12.50 – 15.00
Lady Bug w/Newspaper...$10.00 – 12.50
Lady Bug Hobo ....$10.00 – 12.50

Page 14

Top Row:
1st and 4th, Man Carrying Dragon-lidded Box, 6⅜"...$22.50 – 25.00 ea.
2nd, Georgia Map Ash Tray ....$12.50 – 15.00
3rd, Knight w/Shield Ash Tray......................................$6.00 – 8.00

2nd Row:
Green Floral Cigarette Box w/Two Ash Trays ....$20.00 – 25.00 set
Violet Cigarette Box w/Two Ash Trays ....$25.00 – 30.00 set
Dragon Decoration Cigarette Box w/Two Ash Trays..$25.00 – 35.00 set

3rd Row:
Ash Tray in Hummel-like Design.................................$10.00 – 12.50
Ash Tray to match first box in second row...................$2.00 – 3.00
Children in House Ash Tray ....$4.00 – 5.00
Ash Tray to match second box in row above.................$2.50 – 4.00
Chicken Ash Tray ....$5.00 – 6.00
Ash Tray to match third box in second row..................$3.00 – 5.00

4th Row:
Cigarette Box w/Pink Rose ....$10.00 – 12.50
"Loop over Great Smokies"...$10.00 – 12.50
Diamond Ash Tray...$2.00 – 3.00
Coal Hod Match Holder..$10.00 – 12.50

Coal Hod Match Holder w/Floral Scene.....................$10.00 – 12.50
Moss and Rose Cigarette Box ....$8.00 – 10.00

5th Row:
Pink Embossed Rose Cigarette Box ....$10.00 – 12.50
Blue Floral Cigarette Box ....$10.00 – 12.50
Swirled Floral Cigarette Box ....$10.00 – 12.50
Florida Ash Tray..$12.50 – 15.00

Page 16

Top Row:
Rust Shoe w/Embossed Flower, 2⅜"............................$6.00 – 8.00
Blue Boot, 3½"...$4.00 – 5.00
Cowboy Boot, 4⅜"...$6.00 – 8.00
Boot, 6½" ....$10.00 – 12.50
Tulip Boot ....$6.00 – 8.00
Pink Baby Boot ....$4.00 – 5.00
George Washington Shoe ....$10.00 – 12.50
Ruffled Embossed Flower Shoe...................................$15.00 – 17.50

2nd Row:
1st and 2nd, White Shoes w/Flowers, 1¾" ....$2.50 – 4.00 ea.
3rd, Show w/Rabbit, 2⅜"..$6.00 – 8.00
4th, Dutch Boy w/Shoe ....$8.00 – 10.00
5th, Lady w/Children on Embossed Floral Shoe, 5" h.$75.00 – 85.00
6th, Blue Floral Shoe ....$6.00 – 8.00
7th, Baby Shoe ....$4.00 – 5.00
8th, White Shoe...$2.50 – 4.00
9th, Blue Embossed Floral Shoe, 3½" ....$7.50 – 10.00

3rd Row:
1st, Souvenir Ky. Dam, Ky...$6.00 – 8.00
2nd, Man's Shoe ....$2.00 – 3.00
3rd, Lady's Shoe ....$2.50 – 4.00
4th and 6th, Baby Booty Planters ....$5.00 – 6.00 ea.
5th, Rabbit Shoes ....$6.00 – 8.00
7th, 9th, and 10th, White or Black Shoes ....$2.50 – 4.00 ea.
8th, Brown Floral Shoe ....$7.50 – 10.00

4th Row:
1st and 3rd, Heeled Shoe, 1¼".......................................$2.50 – 4.00 ea.
2nd, Boot..$2.50 – 4.00
4th, White w/Flowers ....$4.00 – 5.00
5th, Blue w/Pink Flower ....$2.50 – 4.00
6th, 7th, 9th, and 11th, Baskets....................................$4.00 – 5.00 ea.
8th, Urn ....$2.00 – 3.00
10th, Urn w/Fruit ....$5.00 – 6.00
12th, Shoe ....$2.50 – 4.00

5th Row:
1st, 2nd, 6th – 8th, 11th, Baskets ....$4.00 – 5.00 ea.
3rd and 10th, Wreaths and Handle w/Rose...................$2.50 – 4.00 ea.
5th, Cat w/Basket ....$5.00 – 6.00
9th, Small Basket ....$2.00 – 3.00
12th, Shoe w/Heel ....$2.00 – 3.00
13th, Ruffled Shoe ....$4.00 – 5.00

Page 18

Top Row:
1st, Lady w/Blue Hat, 5"...$15.00 – 17.50
2nd, Lady w/Pink Hat, 5"..$15.00 – 17.50
3rd and 4th, Lady w/Fruit and Man w/Flowers, 6⅜"...$40.00 – 50.00 pr.
5th, Man Playing Flute...$15.00 – 17.50

6th, Lady in Blue Dress ....$15.00 – 17.50

2nd Row:
Girl w/Feather in Hair, 4⅜" ....$12.50 – 15.00
Man w/Rake ....$12.50 – 15.00
Bootie...$7.50 – 10.00
Colonial Man in Beige Pants ....$12.50 – 15.00
5th and 6th, Wall Pockets, 3⅝" ....$20.00 – 25.00 pr.

3rd Row:
1st and 2nd, Colonial Man and Lady, 4⅜" ....$30.00 – 35.00 pr.
3rd and 4th, Couple w/Urns, 5" ....$65.00 – 75.00 pr.
5th and 6th, White Couple, 4¼".................................$25.00 – 30.00 pr.

4th Row:
1st and 2nd, Pastoral Couple by Fence, 8⅛" ....$75.00 – 100.00 pr.
3rd, Lamp Couple, 7¼" ....$50.00 – 60.00
4th and 5th, Musician Couple 7⅝" ....$50.00 – 60.00 pr.

Page 20
Top Row:
Dog..$10.00 – 12.50
Lamb ....$6.00 – 8.00
Cow..$6.00 – 8.00
Goat..$6.00 – 8.00
Dog..$8.00 – 10.00

2nd Row:
1st and 2nd, Goats...$6.00 – 8.00 ea.
3rd and 5th, Donkey or Horse.....................................$8.00 – 10.00 ea.
4th, Horse ....$8.00 – 10.00

3rd Row:
1st, 2nd, 6th, Jungle Cats ....$8.00 – 10.00 ea.
3rd and 7th, Leopards ....$10.00 – 12.50 ea.
4th and 5th, Tiger or Lion ....$7.50 – 10.00 ea.

4th Row:
Snowsuited Baby ....$40.00 – 50.00
Nodding Head Donkey ....$25.00 – 30.00
Nodding Head Donkey ....$25.00 – 30.00
Snowsuited Baby ....$40.00 – 50.00

5th Row:
1st, Green Snowsuited Baby ....$25.00 – 30.00
2nd, Yellow Snowsuited Jointed Body Baby ....$30.00 – 40.00
3rd, Red-headed Baby...$30.00 – 40.00
4th, U. S. Navy Doll..$25.00 – 30.00

Page 22
Top Row:
Chair w/Roses, 3" ....$12.50 – 15.00
Couch to match, 3"..$17.50 – 20.00
Chair w/Roses ....$10.00 – 12.50
Stool to match ....$6.00 – 8.00
Dresser ....$12.50 – 15.00
Colonial Scene Couch ....$17.50 – 20.00
Chair to match ....$12.50 – 15.00

2nd Row:
1st and 2nd, Chair and Stool w/Blue Rose ....$17.50 – 20.00 set
3rd and 4th, Chair w/Stool to match ....$10.00 – 12.50 set

5th and 6th, Chair w/Stool to match ....$12.50 – 15.00 set
7th, Clock Chair...$12.50 – 15.00
8th – 10th, Lamps ....$10.00 – 12.50 ea.

3rd Row:
1st and 2nd, Bottles...$4.00 – 5.00 ea.
3rd, GE Philco Refrigerator, 2½" ....$17.50 – 20.00
4th, Matching Cabinet w/Dishes, 2¼" ....$15.00 – 17.50
5th, Matching Stove ....$17.50 – 20.00
6th, Matching Dry Sink, 2" ....$10.00 – 12.50
7th, Tub ....$8.00 – 10.00
8th, Pitcher w/Dragon ....$5.00 – 6.00
9th, Phone ....$7.50 – 10.00
10th, Cup and Saucer ....$6.00 – 8.00

4th Row:
1st, Blue Set on Tray..$17.50 – 20.00
2nd, Tray Set..$20.00 – 22.50
3rd and 5th, Luster Cup ....$3.00 – 5.00 ea.
4th, Luster Sugar w/Lid ....$5.00 – 7.00
5th, Orange Luster Plate ....$4.00 – 5.00
6th, Set: Teapot, Creamer, and Sugar ....$20.00 – 25.00

5th Row:
1st and 2nd, Casserole as described above ....$75.00 – 85.00
3rd, Tiny Set Creamer and Sugar on Tray ....$6.00 – 8.00
4th, Marching Toy Soldiers ....$6.00 – 8.00
5th and 6th, Toy Soldiers on Horse ....$6.00 – 8.00 ea.

Page 24
Top Row:
1st, Boy Playing Accordion ....$7.50 – 10.00
2nd, Boy Playing Bass Fiddle......................................$7.50 – 10.00
3rd, Boy Playing Accordion, 5" ....$10.00 – 12.50
4th and 5th, Girl and Boy Fiddlers ....$8.00 – 10.00 ea.
6th and 7th, Boy Playing Accordion.............................$10.00 – 12.50 ea.
8th, Boy Playing Mandolin ....$10.00 – 12.50

2nd Row:
1st, Girl Playing Accordion w/Dog, 3⅞" ....$10.00 – 12.50
2nd, Boy Playing Accordion w/Dog..............................$10.00 – 12.50
3rd, Girl Playing Accordion ....$6.00 – 8.00
4th and 9th, Fiddlers ....$4.00 – 5.00 ea.
5th and 6th, Boys Playing Fiddle or Mandolin ....$5.00 – 6.00 ea.
7th, Boy Playing Accordion ....$7.50 – 10.00
8th, Boy Playing Accordion ....$6.00 – 8.00

3rd Row:
1st, Boy Playing Accordion, 2⅝" ....$2.00 – 3.00
2nd and 10th, Boy Playing Accordion...........................$2.50 – 4.00 ea.
3rd and 4th, Girl Playing Fiddle & Boy Playing Accordion..$4.00 – 5.00 ea.
5th – 9th, Musicians ....$2.50 – 4.00 ea.

4th Row:
1st, Accordion Playing for Chicken, 4⅛" ....$5.00 – 6.00
2nd, 3rd, and 6th, Violin Playing Fence Sitters ....$6.00 – 8.00 ea.
4th and 5th, Boy Playing Accordion.............................$6.00 – 8.00 ea.
7th, Colonial Boy Holding Violin..................................$6.00 – 8.00
8th, Seated Guitar Player ....$4.00 – 5.00

5th Row:
1st – 3rd, Robed Accordion, Mandolin & Bass Players ..$15.00 – 17.50 ea.

4th, Girl w/Song Book, 5¾" ....$30.00 – 35.00
5th, Boy Playing Accordion...$6.00 – 8.00

Page 26

Top Row:
1st, Flutist, 6" ....$15.00 – 17.50
2nd – 4th, Boys Playing Drums, Tuba, and Horn, 4⅞" .$12.50 – 15.00 ea.
5th, Seated Flutist..$5.00 – 6.00
6th and 8th, Boys Playing Sax and Tuba ....$8.00 – 10.00 ea.
7th, Boy Playing Horn ....$5.00 – 6.00

2nd Row:
Tuba Players, 3½" ....$5.00 – 6.00
Child Seated on Fence ....$6.00 – 8.00
Children on Fence ....$6.00 – 8.00
Boy Playing to Dogs ....$7.50 – 10.00
Seated Player...$6.00 – 8.00
6th – 8th, Seated Horn Players or Drummer...................$2.50 – 4.00 ea.

3rd Row:
1st, 3rd, & 6th, Horn Player for Dogs, Chick, or Goose, 2⅝" .$2.50 – 4.00 ea.
2nd, Seated w/Bird..$4.00 – 5.00
4th, Seated on Fence, 2⅜"...$2.50 – 4.00
5th, Girl w/Yellow Dress ....$6.00 – 8.00
7th, Girl w/Book ....$6.00 – 8.00
8th, Girl w/Umbrella, 4¼" ....$6.00 – 8.00

4th Row:
1st, Seated w/Duck...$12.50 – 15.00
2nd, and 5th, Girl on Fence or w/Umbrella and Dog.......$6.00 – 8.00 ea.
3rd, Seated Girl, 4¾" ....$10.00 – 12.50
4th, Seated Girl (slightly smaller), 4½" ....$10.00 – 12.50
6th, Girl w/Umbrella ....$4.00 – 5.00
7th, Seated girl w/Watering Can...................................$12.50 – 15.00

5th Row:
1st – 3rd, "Dolly Dimples" w/Rabbit or Duck............$10.00 – 12.50 ea.
4th, Girl Holding Doll, 4¼"..$12.50 – 15.00
5th, Girl w/Cloak ....$6.00 – 8.00
6th – 8th, Girls w/Rabbit or Chick................................$4.00 – 5.00 ea.
9th, Girl w/Pocket Book, 4⅛"..$7.50 – 10.00

Page 28

Top Row:
Sets of Green, Blue, and Pink ....$17.50 – 20.00 ea.

2nd Row:
"Capo di Monte"-type Plate...$10.00 – 12.50
Set, w/dancing girls...$20.00 – 25.00
Set, w/dancing girls...$25.00 – 30.00
Demitasse, 1¼" ....$20.00 – 22.50

3rd Row:
Set, red hearts w/black trim ....$7.50 – 10.00
Set, blue w/floral ....$10.00 – 12.50
Set, black w/gold trim ....$10.00 – 12.50
Set, blue and white ....$10.00 – 12.50

4th Row:
Set ....$7.50 – 10.00
Set, black and white checkerboard border ....$4.00 – 5.00
Set, blue rim ....$5.00 – 6.00

Set, Florida souvenir ....$8.00 – 10.00

5th Row:
Set, ladies w/red rim ....$20.00 – 22.50
Set, yellow rim flower..$7.50 – 10.00
Demitasse White Floral..$8.00 – 10.00
Set ....$7.50 – 10.00

Page 30

Top Row:
Demitasse, light yellow w/floral ....$5.00 – 6.00
Demitasse, Oriental scene w/Lady ....$8.00 – 10.00
Demitasse, white w/flowers ....$6.00 – 8.00
Demitasse, cream w/basket weave rim ....$8.00 – 10.00
Demitasse, "Moss Rose" type ....$8.00 – 10.00

2nd Row:
Set, white w/pink ....$6.00 – 8.00
Set, white w/roses ....$6.00 – 8.00
Set, white w/leaves ....$4.00 – 5.00
Set, fancy, footed cup w/daisy ....$7.50 – 10.00

3rd Row:
Demitasse, black w/lacy flower ....$10.00 – 12.50
Demitasse, fancy w/gold, 2⅝" ....$15.00 – 17.50
Demitasse, hexagonal ....$12.50 – 15.00
Demitasse, small dragon ....$10.00 —12.50
Demitasse, large dragon ....$12.50 – 15.00

4th Row:
Demitasse, green stripe ....$12.50 – 15.00
Demitasse, Colonial scene ....$20.00 – 22.50
Demitasse, black and orange floral ....$10.00 – 12.50
Demitasse, Oriental house scene...................................$4.00 – 5.00
Demitasse, wine rim...$6.00 – 8.00

5th Row:
Demitasse, rust swirl ....$10.00 – 12.50
Demitasse, blue rim ....$5.00 – 6.00
Demitasse, orange luster rim ....$5.00 – 6.00
Demitasse, rose w/gold ....$6.00 – 8.00
Demitasse, rust curved in top..$10.00 – 12.50

Page 32

Top Row:
Saucer, black w/orange flower.......................................$2.00 – 3.00
Saucer, green w/orange star shaped flower....................$2.00 – 3.00
Saucer, black Iris...$2.00 – 3.00
Saucer, green w/gold stripe..$2.00 – 3.00

2nd Row:
Saucer, pine cone on gray ....$2.00 – 3.00
Saucer, rust, square ....$2.00 – 3.00
Saucer, green w/rose ....$2.00 – 3.00
Saucer, yellow w/flowers..$2.00 – 3.00

3rd Row:
Demitasse, 1½", violet flowers ....$6.00 – 8.00
Miniature, 1", souvenir Army Navy Hospital ....$6.00 – 8.00
Miniature, white floral ....$7.50 – 10.00
Miniature, squared cup...$8.00 – 10.00
Miniature, scalloped, six sided.......................................$6.00 – 8.00

4th Row:
Miniature, pink blush ....$10.00 – 12.50
Miniature, square floral saucer ....$4.00 – 5.00
Same as 2nd in Row 3 except blue rim and not souvenir $4.00 – 5.00
Miniature, souvenir N.Y.C. and Statue of Liberty...........$6.00 – 8.00
Miniature, green rim floral.............................$5.00 – 6.00

5th Row:
Miniature, blue rim, ⅞" ....$6.00 – 8.00
Miniature, green rim ....$5.00 – 6.00
Miniature, square footed cup ....$6.00 – 8.00
Miniature, gold/white.................................$6.00 – 8.00
Demitasse, "New Orleans, La., Courtyard" ....$8.00 – 10.00

Page 34

Top Row:
Plate, "Niagara Falls"................................$7.50 – 10.00
Plate, "Souvenir of Cheyenne, Wyoming" ....$4.00 – 5.00
Plate, rust dragon ....$5.00 – 6.00
Saucer, blue striped..................................$2.00 – 3.00
Cup, gray, silver, and gold, footed.........................$6.00 – 8.00

2nd Row:
Hanging Plate, "Mackinaw Isl., Mich." ....$2.50 – 4.00
Plate, "Niagara" Falls.................................$4.00 – 5.00
Plate, "Parliament Building, Winnipeg".....................$4.00 – 5.00
Plate, "New Orleans" ....$6.00 – 8.00
Blue Tulip Shaped Cut, "Merit China".......................$8.00 – 10.00
White w/Gold Four-footed Cup ....$8.00 – 10.00

3rd Row:
Plate, windmill scene ....$2.50 – 4.00
Hanging Plate, "Castalia, Ohio" ....$2.50 – 4.00
Cup and Saucer, squared, black ....$8.00 – 10.00
Demitasse Cup Only ....$5.00 – 6.00
Demitasse Cup Only w/Dragon ....$7.50 – 10.00
Miniature Set, w/scene ....$4.00 – 5.00
Miniature set, blue rim, "Grand Canyon" ....$6.00 – 8.00

4th Row:
Miniature Set, green rim ....$4.00 – 5.00
Plate to match..$2.50 – 4.00
Miniature Set, rust rim ....$2.50 – 4.00
Hanging Plate, "Cherokee Indian Reservation, N.C." .....$4.00 – 5.00
Miniature Set, white floral..............................$5.00 – 6.00
Plate, matching square white floral.........................$2.50 – 4.00
Miniature Set, ¾" "Souvenir of Las Vegas, N.M." ....$6.00 – 8.00
Cup, four footed, black ....$10.00 – 12.50

5th Row:
1st, Cup only ....$4.00 – 5.00
2nd – 5th Cups only ....$8.00 – 10.00 ea.

Page 36

Top Row:
1st, Cabin Scene w/Five Chickens............................$17.50 – 20.00
2nd and 3rd, Plums or Cherries.....................$20.00 – 25.00 ea.
4th, Sailing Ship ....$17.50 – 20.00

2nd Row:
Fish Dish ....$10.00 – 12.50
Lake Scene w/Two Buildings ....$6.00 – 8.00

Floral Handled Relish ....$6.00 – 8.00
Lake Scene w/Two Swans ....$10.00 – 12.50
Birds of Paradise w/Luster Edge...........................$12.50 – 15.00

3rd Row:
Geisha Girl Plates ....$20.00 – 25.00 ea.

4th Row:
Brown Leaf w/Handle................................$8.00 – 10.00
Brown, curled finger handle ....$8.00 – 10.00
Brown Divided Dish ....$4.00 – 5.00
Brown w/Grapes and Four Holes for Handles................$6.00 – 8.00

Page 38

Top Row:
Yellow Flower ....$12.50 – 15.00
Scalloped Edge Fruit w/Peach and Plums ....$7.50 – 10.00
Purple Leaf ....$6.00 – 8.00
Orange Flowers ....$12.50 – 15.00
Oval Lattice Bowl ....$10.00 – 12.50

2nd Row:
Rose Floral Dish ....$4.00 – 5.00
"Cup of Gold" ....$10.00 – 12.50
Lattice Ladies w/Child................................$17.50 – 20.00
Shell w/Couple ....$6.00 – 8.00
Blue Edge Floral ....$8.00 – 10.00
Red Edge Floral ....$8.00 – 10.00

3rd Row:
Floral ....$2.50 – 4.00
Leaf Relish ....$10.00 – 12.50
Latticed Floral Bowl ....$6.00 – 8.00
Floral Leaf ....$7.50 – 10.00
Tree Scene.......................................$5.00 – 6.00
Dog..$10.00 – 12.50
Latticed Fruit w/Grapes and Peach ....$8.00 – 10.00

4th Row:
Floral Leaf.......................................$2.50 – 4.00
Latticed Floral ....$6.00 – 8.00
Latticed Fruit and Flowers ....$10.00 – 12.50
Square Floral bowl ....$6.00 – 8.00
Square, Handled Floral Plate ....$8.00 – 10.00
Square, Handled Floral Plate ....$8.00 – 10.00

Page 40

Top Row:
Sugar w/Lid......................................$10.00 – 12.50
8" Vegetable Bowl.................................$15.00 – 17.50
Cereal Bowl ....$5.00 – 6.00
Creamer..$6.00 – 8.00

2nd Row:
Platter, 15" ....$20.00 – 25.00

3rd Row:
Cup and Saucer ....$7.50 – 10.00
Bread and Butter Plate ....$2.50 – 4.00
Dinner Plate ....$20.00 – 22.50
Set for 4..$175.00 – 200.00
Set for 6:...$225.00 – 250.00

Set for 8:...$275.00 – 300.00
Set for 12:...$400.00 – 450.00

Page 42

Top Row:
Saucer...$2.00 – 3.00
Dinner Plate, 9".....................................$12.50 – 15.00
Sugar w/Lid...$17.50 – 20.00
Salad Plate, 7"...$6.00 – 8.00
Creamer...$12.50 – 15.00
Cereal Bowl, 5¾".................................$12.50 – 15.00
Berry Bowl, 4½".....................................$10.00 – 12.50

2nd Row:
Dinner Plate, w/red and yellow flowers.....$17.50 – 20.00
Berry Bowl, same....................................$10.00 – 12.50
Bread and Butter ....$4.00 – 5.00
Dinner Plate ....$10.00 – 12.50
Saucer...$2.00 – 3.00

3rd Row:
Cup and Saucer ....$15.00 – 17.50
Platter, 12" ....$40.00 – 50.00
Berry Bowl ....$10.00 – 12.50
Platter, 12" ....$25.00 – 30.00

Page 44

Top Row:
Sugar w/Lid..$15.00 – 17.50
Creamer, floral as on sugar ....$8.00 – 10.00
Sugar w/Lid..$15.00 – 17.50
Sugar w/Lid..$10.00 – 12.50
Creamer to match ....$6.00 – 8.00
Saucer to match..$2.00 – 3.00

2nd Row:
Creamer...$6.00 – 8.00
Sugar w/Lid to match.............................$10.00 – 12.50
Berry Bowl..$4.00 – 5.00
4th, Berry Bowl...$4.00 – 5.00

3rd Row:
Creamer...$6.00 – 8.00
Sugar w/Lid to match.............................$10.00 – 12.50
Sugar w/Lid..$15.00 – 17.50
Sugar w/Lid..$10.00 – 12.50
Creamer to match ....$6.00 – 8.00

4th Row:
Creamer, small flowers ....$10.00 – 12.50
Sugar w/Lid..$15.00 – 17.50
Creamer to match ....$8.00 – 10.00
Cup ....$4.00 – 5.00
Creamer...$7.50 – 10.00

5th Row:
Snack Sets ....$12.50 – 15.00 ea.
Snack Set w/Cup ....$12.50 – 15.00

Page 46

Top Row:
One-handed Orator Gnome, 5⅛" ....$12.50 – 15.00

Tired Old Gnome ....$10.00 – 12.50
Red Elf w/Pot ....$12.50 – 15.00
Elf w/Log ....$10.00 – 12.50
Red Elf w/Planter.....................................$12.50 – 15.00
Gnome w/Basket......................................$12.50 – 15.00

2nd Row:
1st, Leaf Hat Recliner ....$10.00 – 12.50
2nd and 3rd, Leaf Reclining Pair ....$20.00 – 25.00 pr.
4th, Elf on Frog ....$20.00 – 25.00
5th, Elf on Caterpillar ....$12.50 – 15.00

3rd Row:
1st – 3rd and 6th, Purple Suited Elves ....$12.50 – 15.00 ea.
4th and 5th, Green Suited Elves.................$15.00 – 17.50 ea.

4th Row:
1st and 3rd, Orange Suited Sitters..............$10.00 – 12.50 ea.
2nd and 4th, Purple or Blue Recliners ....$10.00 – 12.50 ea.
5th, Old Lady Gnome, 2½".........................$4.00 – 5.00
6th, Old Lady Gnome, 3¾".........................$6.00 – 8.00
7th and 8th, Old Man Gnome ....$6.00 – 8.00 ea.

5th Row:
1st and 3rd, Wooden Looking Figurines.......$6.00 – 8.00 ea.
2nd and 4th – 8th, Wooden Looking Musicians.............$6.00 – 8.00 ea.

Page 48

Top Row:
Indian Planter, 7⅛" ....$20.00 – 25.00
American Indian Ash Tray........................$10.00 – 12.50
Black Drummer, 5" ....$40.00 – 45.00
Black Horn Player, 6¼" ....$40.00 – 45.00
Cowboy Ash Tray ....$2.50 – 4.00
Mexican on Donkey, 8¼" ....$25.00 – 30.00

2nd Row:
1st – 5th, Black Musicians, 2¾" ....$15.00 – 20.00 ea.
6th and 7th, Dutch Girl and Boy ....$12.50 – 15.00 pr.
8th and 9th, Single Dutch Shakers...............$5.00 – 6.00 ea.

3rd Row:
1st and 2nd, Dutch Girl and Boy ....$20.00 – 25.00 pr.
Dutch Girl Bell..$12.50 – 15.00
Seated Dutch Girl ....$12.50 – 15.00
Seated Dutch Boy ....$12.50 – 15.00
Small Dutch Girl ....$4.00 – 5.00
Dutch Boy ....$5.00 – 6.00
Single Dutch Shaker ....$5.00 – 6.00

4th Row:
American Indian Lady, 4¼"........................$6.00 – 8.00
American Indian in Canoe ....$10.00 – 12.50
Cowgirl on Horse ....$6.00 – 8.00
Cowboy or Mexican Drummer ....$5.00 – 6.00
Cowgirl ....$7.50 – 10.00
Mexican Guitar Player ....$5.00 – 6.00
Cowboy ....$7.50 – 10.00

5th Row:
1st and 2nd, Indian Couple, 6⅛"...............$25.00 – 30.00 pr.
3rd, Organ Grinder...................................$20.00 – 22.50

4th, American Indian Chief, 5¹⁄₁₆" ....$15.00 – 20.00
5th, Hawaiian Girl w/Guitar ....$10.00 – 12.50
6th and 7th, Hula Girls...$7.50 – 10.00 ea.

Page 50

Top Row:
Colonial Couple in Blue, 4¾" ....$12.50 – 15.00
Couple w/Man in Yellow Cape.....................................$20.00 – 22.50
Couple w/Hats...$12.50 – 15.00
Man Whispering in Her Ear ....$25.00 – 30.00
Fence Sitters..$12.50 – 15.00
Mandolin Wooing ....$12.50 – 15.00

2nd Row:
1st, Seated Couple w/Book, 3⅜" ....$10.00 – 12.50
2nd, 4th, and 7th, Couples ....$10.00 – 12.50 ea.
3rd, 5th, and 8th Couples ....$10.00 – 12.50 ea.
6th, Removing or Putting on Coat ....$12.50 – 15.00

3rd Row:
Dancing Couple, 7¼" ....$30.00 – 35.00
Cinderella and Prince Charming..................................$125.00 – 150.00
Couple, 7⅛" ....$30.00 – 35.00
Dancers, 6⅛" ....$25.00 – 30.00

4th Row:
1st, Colonial Seated, 3⅝" ....$7.50 – 10.00
2nd, 5th, and 7th, Couples ....$10.00 – 12.50 ea.
3rd and 4th, Couples, 5½" ....$20.00 – 22.50 ea.
6th, Wooden Looking Couple.......................................$15.00 – 17.50

Page 52

Top Row:
1st and 3rd, Sled Couple, 5¾" ....$175.00 – 200.00 pr.
2nd, Courting Couple, 6¼" ....$40.00 – 50.00

2nd Row:
1st and 4th, Couples, 5½" ....$17.50 – 20.00 ea.
2nd and 3rd, Couples ....$20.00 – 25.00 ea.

3rd Row:
1st and 3rd, Couples, 4" ....$17.50 – 20.00 ea.
2nd, Couple...$10.00 – 12.50
4th, Couple, 5" ....$17.50 – 20.00
5th, Couple..$20.00 – 25.00

4th Row:
Man in Hat, 3¾" ....$15.00 – 17.50
Triple Figure ....$15.00 – 20.00
Seated Couple w/Dog ....$30.00 – 40.00
Musician Lady and Fellow..$20.00 – 25.00
Couple at Piano ....$12.50 – 15.00
Couple...$12.50 – 15.00

5th Row:
Cellist Lady and Fellow, 3½" ....$20.00 – 25.00
Couple w/Dog ....$12.50 – 15.00
Couples, 2⅜"...$4.00 – 5.00
Dancers...$6.00 – 8.00
Couples, 2⅜"...$4.00 – 5.00
Couple...$5.00 – 6.00
Skirt Lifter...$12.50 – 15.00

Page 54

Top Row:
Couple at Piano, 5½" ....$65.00 – 75.00
Lady w/Fan and Man w/Hat, 6⅜"..................................$40.00 – 50.00
Man Wooing Lady w/Flute, 6⅞" ....$65.00 – 75.00

2nd Row:
Couple w/Lady Playing Mandolin, 5½" ....$40.00 – 50.00
Couple w/Man Playing Mandolin..................................$20.00 – 25.00
Seated Couple ....$10.00 – 12.50
Couple...$17.50 – 20.00

3rd Row:
1st and 2nd, Colonial Pair, 4⅛" ....$25.00 – 30.00 pr.
3rd and 4th, Couple Pair ....$30.00 – 35.00 pr.
5th and 6th, Mandolin Playing Man Pair, 4⅜" ....$35.00 – 40.00 pr.

4th Row:
1st and 2nd, Couple, 5" ....$40.00 – 50.00 pr.
3rd and 4th, Couple, 3¾" ....$17.50 – 20.00 pr.
5th and 6th, Slightly different sizes ....$17.50 – 20.00 ea.

5th Row:
1st, Dancing Couple, 3⅛" ....$8.00 – 10.00
2nd – 5th, Couples, 2¼" to 2½".....................................$5.00 – 6.00 ea.
6th, Couple..$12.50 – 15.00
7th, Couple Seated ....$12.50 – 15.00

Page 56

Top Row:
1st and 2nd, Pair, 6¼" ....$45.00 – 60.00
3rd and 4th, Pair, 7½" ....$40.00 – 50.00
5th and 6th, Colonial Pair, 8".......................................$50.00 – 65.00

2nd Row:
1st and 2nd, Pair Dancers, 5¼" ....$30.00 – 35.00
3rd and 4th, Pair w/Baskets, 5½" ....$35.00 – 40.00
5th and 6th, Dutch Pair, 4⅛" ....$20.00 – 22.50
7th and 8th, Colonial Pair, 5½" ....$30.00 – 35.00

3rd Row:
1st and 2nd, Pair Musicians, 10⅛" ....$110.00 – 125.00
3rd and 4th, Pair in Yellow, 10" ....$125.00 – 150.00
5th and 6th, Pair Dutch Peasants, 8¼" ....$50.00 – 65.00

4th Row:
1st and 2nd, Colonial Pair, 6⅛" ....$40.00 – 50.00
3rd and 4th, Colonial Pair, 6½" ....$45.00 – 60.00
5th and 6th, Dutch Pair ....$17.50 – 20.00
7th and 8th, Fancy Laced Pair.....................................$35.00 – 50.00

Page 58

Top Row:
Arms Behind Head Pose, 5" ....$15.00 – 17.50
Holding Hem and Hat ....$17.50 – 20.00
Ballerina with Net Dress, 5¾" ....$35.00 – 40.00
Holding Hem of Dress ....$10.00 – 12.50
Dancing Planter, 5½" ....$12.50 – 15.00

2nd Row:
Green Skirted, 3½"..$10.00 – 12.50
White Skirted ....$5.00 – 6.00

Green and White Dress ....$6.00 – 8.00
Ballerina ....$15.00 – 17.50
Blue Ruffled Skirt ....$7.50 – 10.00
White Skirted w/Rust Top ....$4.00 – 5.00

3rd Row:
Ballerina, 4¾" ....$40.00 – 45.00
Ballerina ....$15.00 – 17.50
Ballerina ....$10.00 – 12.50
Ballerina ....$17.50 – 20.00
Ballerina w/Purple Dress ....$30.00 – 35.00

4th Row:
1st, 3rd and 6th, Small Dancers, 2½".............$5.00 – 6.00 ea.
2nd, Pink, holding dress hems ....$8.00 – 10.00
4th and 5th, Orange Skirt and Blue Top ....$5.00 – 6.00 ea.
7th, White w/Gold..$6.00 – 8.00

5th Row:
1st and 6th, Yellow Skirt, 3½".......................$8.00 – 10.00 ea.
2nd and 5th, 5⅜" ....$20.00 – 25.00 ea.
3rd, Hands Behind Head Pose ....$15.00 – 17.50
4th, Windswept Lady ....$12.50 – 15.00

Page 60

Top Row:
Lady w/Tambourine, 4¾".................................$6.00 – 8.00
Lady in White and Gold.................................$8.00 – 10.00
Lady w/Rust Top...$6.00 – 8.00
Lady w/Feathered Hat, 6" ....$10.00 – 12.50
Mexican Lady, 7¼"..$35.00 – 40.00
Lady Holding Hat ....$10.00 – 12.50
Lady in Yellow and Blue Dress ....$12.50 – 15.00
Lady w/Basket ....$8.00 – 10.00

2nd Row:
1st, Surprised Expression, 5" ....$12.50 – 15.00
2nd, Holding Green Dress..............................$10.00 – 12.50
3rd, Yellow Top w/Bow in Hair ....$5.00 – 6.00
4th, Lady w/Rust Top ....$6.00 – 8.00
5th, Lady Holding Hat ....$12.50 – 15.00
6th, 7th, 9th, and 10th, Ladies.......................$10.00 – 12.50 ea.
8th, Lady in Pink and Blue ....$2.50 – 4.00

3rd Row:
1st, Lady w/Scottie, 4½"...............................$12.50 – 15.00
2nd and 7th, Lady in White and Seated Lady.............$10.00 – 12.50 ea.
3rd and 4th, Ladies in Yellow Floral Skirts................$15.00 – 17.50 ea.
5th, Lady Reading Book, 5".............................$22.50 – 25.00
6th, Crinoline Dress Lady, 5⅝" ....$35.00 – 40.00

4th Row:
Lady w/Crown and Scepter, 8⅛" ....$40.00 – 45.00
Lady Reading Book, 8⅜".................................$30.00 – 35.00
Buxom Lady Holding Fan 9¾"..........................$45.00 – 50.00
Dutch Lady w/Flowers, 10⅛"...........................$40.00 – 50.00
Girl w/Apron, 8¼"..$30.00 – 35.00
Well Endowed Dancer ....$20.00 – 25.00

Page 62

Top Row:
Blue Boy, 7⅝"..$30.00 – 35.00

Man in Striped Pants.....................................$20.00 – 25.00
Peasant ....$15.00 – 20.00
Scratching Head ....$15.00 – 17.50
Man in Pink Pants ....$17.50 – 20.00
Plaid Shirt and Blue Pants.............................$17.50 – 20.00
Colonial Man ....$17.50 – 20.00
Man w/Hand to Lips ....$10.00 – 12.00

2nd Row:
1st, Sharp dresser, 5"....................................$10.00 – 12.50
2nd, White w/Brownish Finish ....$10.00 – 12.50
3rd, 7th, 8th, and 10th, Men.............................$6.00 – 8.00 ea.
4th, Colonial Man ....$6.00 – 8.00
5th and 6th, Men ....$10.00 – 12.50 ea.
9th, Colonial...$5.00 – 6.00

3rd Row:
1st, Flute Player, 5".......................................$8.00 – 10.00
2nd, 7th, and 8th, Men ....$7.50 – 10.00 ea.
3rd, 4th, and 6th, Men ....$6.00 – 8.00 ea.
5th, Man in Yellow Coat ....$5.00 – 6.00
9th, Seated Man ....$4.00 – 5.00
10th, White w/Brown ....$7.50 – 10.00

4th Row:
1st and 5th, Colonial Men, 4" ....$6.00 – 8.00 ea.
2nd and 3rd, Musketeer and Colonial ....$5.00 – 6.00 ea.
4th, 7th, and 8th, Colonial Men ....$2.50 – 4.00 ea.
6th, Man w/Hat Under Arm ....$5.00 – 6.00
9th, Fiddler ....$7.50 – 10.00
10th, Guitar Player ....$10.00 – 12.50

5th Row:
1st, Man Bowing, 6" ....$20.00 – 22.50
2nd, Man w/Basket ....$12.50 – 15.00
3rd and 7th, Colonial Men ....$15.00 – 17.50 ea.
4th and 6th, Musicians ....$17.50 – 20.00 ea.
5th, Cowboy ....$15.00 – 17.50
8th, Man w/Yellow Cape ....$12.50 – 15.00

Page 64

Top Row:
1st, Lady w/Fan, 5".......................................$10.00 – 12.50
2nd and 8th, Seated or Standing Girls ....$8.00 – 10.00 ea.
3rd, Dancer, 6¾"..$15.00 – 17.50
4th, Black P. J. ....$10.00 – 12.50
5th, Fan Lady ....$15.00 – 17.50
6th, Lady w/Goose ....$15.00 – 17.50
7th, Little Guy ....$7.50 – 10.00

2nd Row:
1st and 2nd, Girl w/Fan and Boy w/Blue Top, 4"............$6.00 – 8.00 ea.
3rd, Smaller version of 2nd............................$4.00 – 5.00
4th, 5th, & 8th, Girl w/Fan, Man w/Flute, Boy w/Pig.$10.00 – 12.50 ea.
6th, Guy(?) ....$8.00 – 10.00
7th, Folded Hands, 5⅞"..................................$15.00 – 17.50

3rd Row:
1st, Lady w/Fan, 7½" ....$12.50 – 15.00
2nd and 3rd, Ladies w/Fan ....$12.50 – 15.00 ea.
4th, Gray Lady w/Fan, 8"................................$15.00 – 17.50
5th and 6th, Couple, 8¼" ....$40.00 – 50.00 pr.

7th, Dancer, 8" ....$22.50 – 25.00
8th, Mandolin Player ....$10.00 – 12.50

4th Row:
1st and 2nd, Figurines, 7" ....$12.50 – 15.00 ea.
3rd, Lady w/Basket on Head, 7⅞" ....$20.00 – 25.00
4th, Man w/Hands in Sleeves ....$20.00 – 22.50
5th and 6th, Matching bases and marks ....$17.50 – 20.00 ea.
7th, Similar to 1st and 2nd ....$12.50 – 15.00
8th, Warrior ....$12.50 – 15.00

Page 66

Top Row:
Pink Hatted Girl w/Baskets, 5⅛" ....$15.00 – 17.50
Similar to 1st, 6" ....$12.50 – 15.00
3rd and 4th, Boys Holding Hats ....$12.50 – 15.00 ea.

2nd Row:
1st and 2nd, Couple w/Boy Playing a Mandolin ....$25.00 – 30.00 pr.
3rd and 4th, Wall Plaques ....$35.00 – 45.00 pr.
5th and 7th, Violin and Tambourine Players ....$8.00 – 10.00 ea.
6th, Mandolin Player ....$8.00 – 10.00

3rd Row:
All ....$8.00 – 10.00 ea.

4th Row:
1st, Fan Girl, 4⅝" ....$7.50 – 10.00
2nd – 6th, All bisque ranging from 4" to 4⅝" ....$10.00 – 12.50 ea.

5th Row:
1st, Same as 1st in row above except 4⅛" ....$6.00 – 8.00
2nd – 9th, All 4⅛" ....$7.50 – 10.00 ea.

Page 68

Top Row:
1st – 3rd, Chinese Busts ....$25.00 – 30.00 ea.
4th and 5th, Wooden Ship Bookends ....$65.00 – 75.00 pr.

2nd Row:
Girl Head Vase ....$30.00 – 35.00
Lady Vase ....$25.00 – 30.00
Lady Bust ....$17.50 – 20.00
Bird in Tree Bud Vase ....$6.00 – 8.00
Lady Head Vase ....$30.00 – 35.00
Boy Head Vase ....$25.00 – 30.00
Oriental Girl Vase ....$20.00 – 25.00

3rd Row:
1st, Oriental Man Jar w/Lid ....$22.50 – 25.00
2nd and 3rd, Women Heads ....$15.00 – 17.50
4th, Mandolin Player ....$5.00 – 6.00
5th, Angel w/Drum ....$5.00 – 6.00
6th, Angel w/Accordion ....$5.00 – 6.00
7th, Swan-handled Sugar w/Lid ....$45.00 – 50.00
    Lid only ....$20.00 – 22.50
8th, Swan-handled Creamer ....$25.00 – 30.00

4th Row:
Sea Shell Planter ....$10.00 – 12.50
Bird Tile ....$30.00 – 35.00
Cornucopia ....$30.00 – 35.00

4th – 5th, Card Holders ....$15.00 – 17.50 ea.

5th Row:
1st, Small Boy with Missing Top ....$5.00 – 6.00
2nd, Floral Ring Box ....$12.50 – 15.00
3rd, "Wedgwood"-style Ring Box ....$17.50 – 20.00
4th and 5th White Tiles ....$12.50 – 15.00 ea.
6th, Heat-shaped Ring Box ....$12.50 – 15.00
7th, Hexagonal Box w/Embossed Flower ....$10.00 – 12.50

Page 70

Top Row:
1st and 2nd, Courting Couple, 6½" ....$50.00 – 60.00 pr.
3rd, Basket Carrier, 8⅛" ....$30.00 – 35.00
4th, Cowboy, 7⅜" ....$30.00 – 35.00

2nd Row:
1st and 2nd White w/Gold Colonials, 7⅜" ....$55.00 – 65.00 pr.
3rd, Oriental Reading Book ....$30.00 – 35.00

3rd Row:
Pink Hatted Lady, 8⅛" ....$30.00 – 35.00
Seated Bisque Couple ....$65.00 – 75.00
Lady Lifting Skirt ....$30.00 – 35.00

Page 72

Top Row:
New York Crumb Pan ....$10.00 – 12.50
Ornate Swan Crumb Pan ....$17.50 – 20.00
Floral Crumb Pan ....$10.00 – 12.50
Small floral Crumb Pan ....$5.00 – 6.00

2nd Row:
Ash Tray, St. Joseph ....$2.50 – 4.00
Ash Tray, Birmingham ....$2.50 – 4.00
Ash Tray, Boys Town ....$6.00 – 8.00
Ash Tray, Sailboat ....$2.50 – 4.00
Ash Tray, Football ....$5.00 – 6.00

3rd Row:
Ash Tray, Pikes Peak ....$2.50 – 4.00
Ash Tray, Wisconsin Dells ....$2.50 – 4.00
Ash Tray, New York City ....$10.00 – 12.50
Ash Tray, Washington, D.C. ....$2.50 – 4.00

4th Row:
Ash Tray, Hollywood ....$2.50 – 4.00
Ash Tray, Hannibal, Mo. ....$2.50 – 4.00
Ash Tray, Washington, D.C. ....$2.50 – 4.00
Ash Tray, Long Beach ....$2.50 – 4.00

5th Row:
Buddha Box ....$25.00 – 30.00
Pagoda Box ....$25.00 – 30.00
Cupid Box ....$20.00 – 25.00
Red Box w/Sterling Silver Decoration ....$20.00 – 25.00

Page 74

Top Row:
Ash Tray, Alaska ....$10.00 – 12.50
Ash Tray, Colorado ....$2.50 – 4.00
Ash Tray, Chicago ....$2.50 – 4.00

Ash Tray, leaf w/grapes ....$2.50 – 4.00
Ash Tray, Washington, D.C. ....$10.00 – 12.50

2nd Row:
1st, 3rd – 6th, Cigarette Urns ....$5.00 – 6.00 ea.
2nd, Creamer ....$7.50 – 10.00
7th, Hand Ash Tray ....$10.00 – 12.50

3rd Row:
1st and 9th, Creamer and Sugar ....$15.00 – 17.50 pr.
2nd – 8th, Gods ....$12.50 – 15.00 ea.

4th Row:
1st, San Francisco Trolley.............................$20.00 – 22.50
2nd, Small Sugar ....$8.00 – 10.00
3rd and 4th, Cigarette Urns ....$5.00 – 6.00 ea.
5th, Creamer...$10.00 – 12.50
6th – 8th, Saki Glasses or Small Urns...........$6.00 – 8.00 ea.

5th Row:
Pegasus Embossed Box...................................$15.00 – 17.50
Crown Embossed Box......................................$12.50 – 15.00
Silent Butler ....$20.00 – 22.50
Horse Ash Tray ....$15.00 – 17.50
Pegasus Embossed Box...................................$15.00 – 17.50

Page 76

Top Row:
Gun Lighter w/Pearl Handles.........................$15.00 – 17.50
Gun Lighter on Tripod....................................$12.50 – 15.00
Small Gun Lighter...$7.50 – 10.00
Large Gun Lighter on Base.............................$17.50 – 20.00
Small Pearl Handle Lighter.............................$8.00 – 10.00
Pearl Handle Lighter on Base ....$12.50 – 15.00
Gun Lighter on Base ....$8.00 – 10.00

2nd Row:
Baby Table Lighter in Box ....$5.00 – 6.00
Hand Lighter ....$12.50 – 15.00
Champagne Bucket Lighter ....$15.00 – 17.50
Urn Lighter..$8.00 – 10.00
Pin Lighter w/Jewels and Pearls ....$15.00 – 20.00
Gun Lighter ....$6.00 – 8.00
Gun Lighter with Base ....$8.00 – 10.00
Gun Lighter ....$10.00 – 12.50
Pearl Handle Gun Lighter ....$10.00 – 12.50

3rd Row:
1st Bottle Lighter ....$6.00 – 8.00
2nd and 3rd, Genie Lamps ....$12.50 – 15.00 ea.
4th, Basket of Fruit ....$10.00 – 12.50
5th and 6th, Set ....$25.00 – 30.00 set
4th Row:
1st, Heart Ring Box...$10.00 – 12.50
2nd, Silent Butler, paper label.......................$7.50 – 10.00
3rd, Box...$8.00 – 10.00
4th, Cornucopia on Tray, both.......................$15.00 – 17.50 set
5th, Horse Head Ash Tray ....$10.00 – 12.50

5th Row:
1st, Large Book Box ....$12.50 – 15.00
2nd, Small Book Box ....$10.00 – 12.50

3rd – 5th, Piano Boxes....................................$15.00 – 20.00 ea.
6th, Piano Box...$15.00 – 17.50
7th, Piano Box...$12.50 – 15.00

Page 78

Top Row:
Plate Stand ....$10.00 – 15.00
Planter ....$8.00 – 10.00
Owl Planter..$10.00 – 12.50

2nd Row:
1st, Piano ....$7.50 – 10.00
2nd, Pot Belly Stove ....$8.00 – 10.00
3rd and 4th, Small Horses ....$6.00 – 8.00 ea.
5th, Bird on Tree ....$7.50 – 10.00

3rd Row:
Cucumber ....$6.00 – 8.00
Pea Pod..$6.00 – 8.00

4th Row:
Six-piece Tool Set, original card ....$50.00 – 60.00
Army of Occupation Medal ....$40.00 – 50.00
3rd and 4th, Cup Racks...................................$5.00 – 6.00 ea.

5th Row:
Inflatable Rubber Rooster...............................$17.50 – 20.00
Inflatable Rubber Chicken ....$17.50 – 20.00
3rd and 4th, Fuzzy Roosters...........................$10.00 – 12.50 ea.

Page 80

Top Row:
Coaster ....$2.50 – 4.00
Round Serving Plate ....$7.50 – 10.00
Rectangular Tray...$15.00 – 17.50
Small Rectangular Tray ....$7.50 – 10.00
Box of Eight Coasters.....................................$30.00 – 35.00

2nd Row:
1st, Box of Eight Coasters ....$30.00 – 35.00
2nd and 7th, Paper Birds................................$15.00 – 20.00 ea.
3rd, Coaster...$2.50 – 4.00
4th, Red Round Serving Plate ....$7.50 – 10.00
5th, Small Rectangular Tray ....$7.50 – 10.00
6th, Souvenir Plate ....$10.00 – 12.50

3rd Row:
Pink Barn ....$20.00 – 22.50
Red Bowl ....$12.50 – 15.00
American Flag..$1.50 – 2.00 ea.
Small Rectangular Tray ....$7.50 – 10.00
Green Church ....$20.00 – 22.50
Black Round Serving Plate ....$7.50 – 10.00
Blue House...$20.00 – 22.50

Page 82

Top Row:
"Wedgwood"-style Pitcher, 2⅝".....................$8.00 – 10.00
"Wedgwood"-style Pitcher ....$10.00 – 12.50
"Wedgwood"-style Pitcher, 4¼".....................$17.50 – 20.00
Floral Pitcher..$10.00 – 12.50
Floral Pitcher..$12.50 – 15.00

Narrow Neck Embossed Flower Pitcher.......................$7.50 – 10.00
Pitcher ....$5.00 – 6.00

2nd Row:
Basket...$6.00 – 8.00
Basket...$5.00 – 6.00
Blue Wicker Basket ....$6.00 – 8.00
Wishing Well ....$10.00 – 12.50
Basket w/Embossed Flower...................................$4.00 – 5.00
Lady w/Two Baskets..$40.00 – 45.00

3rd Row:
Wheelbarrow w/Roses, 1⅝" x 5".........................$8.00 – 10.00
Wheelbarrow w/Cherry...$6.00 – 8.00
Wheelbarrow w/Yellow Flower.............................$4.00 – 5.00
Blue Wheelbarrow ....$4.00 – 5.00
White Wheelbarrow ....$2.50 – 4.00

4th Row:
1st – 3rd, Suitcase, 2"....................................$4.00 – 5.00 ea.
4th, Basket w/Grapes ....$6.00 – 8.00
5th, Basket w/Roses ....$6.00 – 8.00
6th, Bird handled Basket.....................................$8.00 – 10.00

5th Row:
Blue Basket, 2" ....$3.50 – 5.00
Open Teapot...$2.50 – 4.00
Coffee w/Lid..$6.00 – 8.00
Teapot w/Lid..$6.00 – 8.00
Blue Coffee Pot w/Lid ....$6.00 – 8.00
Teapot w/Lid, embossed rose ....$6.00 – 8.00
Teapot w/Lid..$6.00 – 8.00

Page 84
Top Row:
Brown Dog Planter, 3⅝".......................................$3.00 – 4.00
Black Dog Planter, 4⅝" ....$5.00 – 6.00
Same, orange..$5.00 – 6.00
Same, blue..$5.00 – 6.00
Same as 1st, black ....$3.00 – 4.00

2nd Row:
Brown Dog, 3⅝", w/Top Hat Planter....................$6.00 – 8.00
Same, black and white ....$6.00 – 8.00
Dog Planter ....$17.50 – 20.00
Spotted Dog w/Basket Planter ....$5.00 – 6.00
Dog w/Spotted Basket Planter ....$6.00 – 8.00

3rd Row:
Dog w/Blue Ribbon and Planter ....$5.00 – 6.00
Dog w/Jaws Tied, 1½"...$5.00 – 6.00
Same, only 2⅝"...$7.50 – 10.00
Dog w/Green Basket Planter..................................$6.00 – 8.00
Dog Resting on Sack..$6.00 – 8.00
Pair of Dogs...$6.00 – 8.00
Dog at Fire Plug ....$8.00 – 10.00

4th Row:
Standing Dog ....$17.50 – 20.00
Bird Dog...$7.50 – 10.00
Dog Holding Ball...$7.50 – 10.00
Dog Holding Ball...$10.00 – 12.50

Setter ....$12.50 – 15.00
Bull Dog...$17.50 – 20.00

5th Row:
Begging Dog ....$2.50 – 4.00
Dog w/Blue Ribbon ....$5.00 – 6.00
Spotted Dog ....$6.00 – 8.00
Bull Dog in Red Hat ....$12.50 – 15.00
Brown Dog...$6.00 – 8.00
Group of Three Dogs...$15.00 – 17.50
Sitting Dog..$12.50 – 15.00
Dog w/Bug on Nose..$7.50 – 10.00
Poodle w/Rose Hat..$17.50 – 20.00

Page 86
Top Row:
Donkey w/Green Cart Planter..............................$12.50 – 15.00
Donkey w/Floral Cart Planter ....$7.50 – 10.00
Donkey w/Brown Cart Planter.............................$8.00 – 10.00

2nd Row:
Donkey w/Cart Planter..$10.00 – 12.50
Pack Mule Planter...$10.00 – 12.50
Same as above with different coloring.................$10.00 – 12.50

3rd Row:
Donkey w/Cart Planter..$6.00 – 8.00
Donkey w/Cart Planter..$6.00 – 8.00
Siesta Time w/Donkey Planter............................$12.50 – 15.00

4th Row:
Donkey Pulling Cart Planters.........................$7.50 – 10.00 ea.

5th Row:
1st, Donkey w/Two Basket Planters ....$5.00 – 6.00
2nd, Zebra w/Basket Planter..................................$6.00 – 8.00
3rd, Blue Stripped Donkey w/Two Baskets...........$6.00 – 8.00
4th and 5th, Zebras w/Basket.........................$5.00 – 6.00 ea.
6th, Spotted Horse (?) w/Basket ....$5.00 – 6.00

Page 88
Top Row:
Lady Duck in Bonnet Planter...............................$12.50 – 15.00
Male Duck in Top Hat Planter ....$12.50 – 15.00
Chicken Pitcher..$22.50 – 25.00
Mallard Planter..$12.50 – 15.00

2nd Row:
Cygnet Planter..$8.00 – 10.00
Swan Planter..$12.50 – 15.00
Swan Planter w/Wings Spread.............................$15.00 – 17.50

3rd Row:
Chickens on Planter ....$5.00 – 6.00
Mallard Planter..$10.00 – 12.50
Chicken w/Egg Planter ....$15.00 – 17.50
Chick w/Basket Planter..$5.00 – 6.00

4th Row:
Barnyard Goose Planter...$6.00 – 8.00
Rooster Pulling Egg Cart Planter.........................$17.50 – 20.00
Blue Swan ....$8.00 – 10.00

5th Row:
1st, Green Geese Planter...$12.50 – 15.00
2nd, Goose and Goslings Planter ....$15.00 – 17.50
3rd, Duckling w/Basket Planter ....$6.00 – 8.00
4th, Flamingo w/Basket Planter..................................$10.00 – 12.50

Page 90

Top Row:
Oriental Girl w/Shell Planter, 6⅛".............................$22.50 – 25.00
Tulip Gal Planter..$8.00 – 10.00
Large Hatted Girl Planter...$12.50 – 15.00
Rickshaw Boy Planter...$15.00 – 17.50

2nd Row:
Accordion Player w/Dog Planter, 4⅛".........................$10.00 – 12.50
Lady Planter...$5.00 – 6.00
Girl w/Dried Floral Arrangement ....$6.00 – 8.00
Dutch Couple Planter ....$8.00 – 10.00
Girl w/Dog Planter...$8.00 – 10.00
Couple on Bench Planter ....$7.50 – 10.00
Child Playing Violin on Fence Planter ....$8.00 – 10.00

3rd Row:
Girl w/Mandolin Planter, 3⅝"......................................$7.50 – 10.00
Girl w/Horse Cart Planter ....$5.00 – 6.00
Girl w/Basket Planter..$7.50 – 10.00
Duck Chasing Girl at Wall Planter ....$10.00 – 12.50
Dutch Guy Planter..$10.00 – 12.50
Matching Dutch Girl Planter..$10.00 – 12.50

4th Row:
1st and 2nd, Girl w/Shell Planter, 2¾" ....$5.00 – 6.00 ea.
3rd, Oriental Boy w/Basket...$5.00 – 6.00
4th, Boy on Fence ....$7.50 – 10.00
5th, Colonial w/Basket..$5.00 – 6.00
6th, Mexican Planter ....$5.00 – 6.00
7th, Napping Musician..$6.00 – 8.00

5th Row:
Boy w/Cherry Tree, 3⅝"...$7.50 – 10.00
Shepherd Planter..$7.50 – 10.00
Boy w/Bird Planter ....$6.00 – 8.00
Boy w/Fiddle...$7.50 – 10.00
Umbrella Boy ....$8.00 – 10.00
Red Hooded Lady Planter, 4⅝" ....$8.00 – 10.00

Page 92

Top Row:
Oriental Girl w/Fan Planter, 6⅛" ....$10.00 – 12.50
Man with Vase ....$5.00 – 6.00
Man with Bucket Planters, 6¾" ....$20.00 – 22.50
Girl Musician Planter ....$7.50 – 10.00
Oriental Man matching 1st girl ....$10.00 – 12.50

2nd Row:
Boy Skier Planter, 3⅜", Girl w/Book ....$7.50 – 10.00 ea.
Girl on Bench...$8.00 – 10.00
Boy Planter...$7.50 – 10.00
Oriental Boy w/Basket, Matching Girl to 5th...............$8.00 – 10.00 ea.

3rd Row:
1st and 2nd, Boy and Girl w/Cart, 2⅝"..........................$5.00 – 6.00 ea.

3rd and 4th, Boy and Girl at Well.................................$5.00 – 6.00 ea.
5th, Two Children w/Wheeled Cart Planter....................$6.00 – 8.00
6th, Boy w/Horn Planter ....$7.50 – 10.00

4th Row:
Boy w/Rickshaw Planter..$10.00 – 12.50
Oriental Girl w/Fan Planter...$12.50 – 15.00
Girl w/Dog Planter, 4⅝" ....$12.50 – 15.00
Boy Musician Planter..$8.00 – 10.00
Dutch Boy Planter...$10.00 – 12.50
Boy w/Cart Planter..$12.50 – 15.00

5th Row:
Musician w/Dog Planter, 4⅛".......................................$10.00 – 12.50
Man Walking Donkey Cart Planter................................$6.00 – 8.00
Boy w/Lamb Planter, 5"..$12.50 – 15.00
Girl w/Goose Planter...$5.00 – 6.00
Girl w/Basket ....$5.00 – 6.00
Oriental w/Large Hat Planter ....$7.50 – 10.00

Page 94

Top Row:
Sewn Dog Planter, 5¾"...$10.00 – 12.50
Dogs with Doghouse Planter ....$20.00 – 22.50
Dog Pencil Holder...$7.50 – 10.00
Dog Vase...$10.00 – 12.50
5th and 6th, Lounging Dog Planters ....$5.00 – 7.00 ea.

2nd Row:
1st, Dog in Barrel Planter..$5.00 – 6.00
2nd and 3rd, Dog w/Tree Stump Vase...........................$5.00 – 6.00 ea.
4th, Dog w/Basket...$6.00 – 8.00
5th, Dog w/Pitcher ....$6.00 – 8.00
6th and 7th, Dog w/Hat or Cart.....................................$5.00 – 6.00 ea.
8th, Small Vase w/Bust..$7.50 – 10.00
9th and 10th, Vase w/Birds in Relief ....$15.00 – 17.50 ea.

3rd Row:
Cat Watching Bird Vase ....$12.50 – 15.00
Black Cat Vases ....$10.00 – 12.50 ea.
Cat w/Vase ....$8.00 – 10.00
Donkey w/Cart ....$2.50 – 4.00
Deer w/Basket ....$4.00 – 5.00
Swan Planter ....$5.00 – 6.00

4th Row:
1st and 2nd, Owl on Branch...$10.00 – 12.50 ea.
3rd and 4th, Chicks Vase ....$5.00 – 6.00 ea.
5th Ducks Vase ....$6.00 – 7.00
6th, Squirrel Watching Rooster.....................................$12.50 – 15.00
7th, Squirrel Vase..$7.50 – 10.00
8th, Bird w/Hat Vase...$6.00 – 8.00

5th Row:
1st – 4th, "Wedgwood"-style Vases, 2¾"......................$7.50 – 10.00 ea.
5th, "Wedgwood"-style Vase w/Lady and Cupids ......$10.00 – 12.50
6th – 8th, Colonial Dressed People Vases ....$5.00 6.00 ea.
9th and 10th, Martha & George Washington Vases ....$15.00 – 17.50 ea.

Page 96

Top Row:
1st, Clown Crouching on Drum.....................................$35.00 – 40.00

2nd, Clown on Back on Drum ....$35.00 – 40.00
3rd and 4th, Cat Pair ....$15.00 – 17.50
5th and 6th, Hat Pair ....$12.50 – 15.00 pr.

2nd Row:
1st, Six-piece Colonial Scene Set ....$25.00 – 30.00 set
2nd and 3rd, Dutch Couple ....$12.50 – 15.00 pr.
4th, Three-piece Flowers on Basket............................$15.00 – 20.00

3rd Row:
1st and 2nd, Totem Pole Set ....$10.00 – 12.50 pr.
3rd and 4th, Mugs ....$12.50 – 15.00 pr.
5th and 6th, Pigs...$12.50 – 15.00 pr.
7th and 8th, Squirrels ....$12.50 – 15.00 pr.

4th Row:
(All singles, so double price for pair)
Toadstool..$6.00 – 7.50
Mexican Lady ....$6.00 – 7.50
"Hummel-like" Boy ....$6.00 – 7.50
Dutch Girl ....$6.00 – 7.50
Boy w/Lederhosen ....$5.00 – 6.00
Geisha w/Fan ....$7.50 – 10.00
"Hummel-like" Boy, 4⅜" ....$7.50 – 10.00
Bird ....$5.00 – 6.00
Dutch Boy Bust ....$6.00 – 7.50

5th Row:
Toby Winker ....$10.00 – 12.50
Popeye...$17.50 – 20.00
Duck ....$6.00 – 7.50
Dutch Girl ....$6.00 – 7.50
Cowboy ....$7.50 – 10.00
Strawberry...$5.00 – 6.00
Seated Dutch Girl..$6.00 – 8.00
Paddling Indian ....$6.00 – 7.50

Page 98

Top Row:
Honeycomb Design Creamer, 2⅝" ....$10.00 – 12.50
Sugar w/Lid to match...$17.50 – 20.00
Beehive Teapot w/Honeycomb Design ....$35.00 – 40.00
Beehive Honey Jar ....$22.50 – 25.00
Bee Two-part Relish ....$17.50 – 20.00

2nd Row:
1st, Honeycomb Creamer, 2¾" ....$12.50 – 15.00
2nd – 4th, Three-piece Set ....$20.00 – 22.50 set
5th, Marmalade Hive ....$15.00 – 17.50
6th, Honeycomb Design Sugar w/Lid..............................$20.00 – 22.50
7th, Honeycomb Design Honey Jar ....$17.50 – 20.00
8th, Salt and Pepper w/Holder ....$15.00 – 17.50 set

3rd Row:
1st, Cottage Creamer, 2⅝" ....$12.50 – 15.00
2nd, Cottage Creamer, 2" ....$10.00 – 12.50
3rd, Large Sugar to match 1st creamer ....$22.50 – 25.00
4th and 5th, Salt and Pepper ....$17.50 – 20.00 pr.
6th, Sugar to match 2nd creamer ....$15.00 – 17.50

4th Row:
Tomato Sugar...$15.00 – 17.50

Tomato Cracker or Biscuit Jar ....$75.00 – 85.00
Tomato Sugar...$15.00 – 17.50

Page 100

Top Row:
Dragon Creamer...$15.00 – 17.50
Dragon Sugar w/Lid...$25.00 – 27.50
Dragon Demitasse Cup and Saucer................................$17.50 – 20.00
Flat Bottomed Cup ....$12.50 – 15.00
Dragon Demitasse Pot ....$75.00 – 85.00
Seventeen-piece set as shown ....$235.00 – 265.00

2nd Row:
Teapot, blue trimmed floral ....$30.00 – 35.00
Teapot, floral ....$45.00 – 50.00
Embossed Dragon Teapot ....$100.00 – 125.00
Dragon Teapot ....$85.00 – 100.00

3rd Row:
1st and 5th, Floral Demitasse Cup and Saucer ....$12.50 – 15.00 set
2nd, Floral Creamer ....$15.00 – 17.50
3rd, Demitasse Pot ....$65.00 – 75.00
4th, Floral Sugar w/Lid ....$22.50 – 27.50
Seventeen-piece set as shown ....$190.00 – 215.00

4th Row:
Brown Teapot w/Embossed Flowers ....$30.00 – 35.00
Brown Individual Teapot ....$20.00 – 22.50
Blue Stoneware Teapot w/Bamboo Handle..........................$25.00 – 30.00
Brown Teapot w/Embossed Flowers ....$35.00 – 40.00

Page 102

Top Row:
1st and 5th, Plate, "Noritake" ....$10.00 – 12.50 ea.
2nd, Creamer, "Noritake" ....$17.50 – 20.00
3rd, Teapot, "Noritake".......................................$50.00 – 55.00
4th, Sugar w/Lid, "Noritake" ....$25.00 – 27.50

2nd Row:
1st and 3rd, Cup and Saucer to match 1st row...................$12.50 – 15.00 ea.
2nd, Floral Teapot...$30.00 – 35.00

3rd Row:
Sugar w/Lid..$30.00 – 35.00
Teapot w/Lid...$75.00 – 85.00
Creamer ....$20.00 – 25.00

4th Row:
1st, Brown Two-cup Teapot ....$15.00 – 17.50
2nd – 8th, Rust Dragon Saki Set................................$85.00 – 100.00
Saki Cup w/Lithopane Geisha Girl...............................$8.00 – 10.00 ea.
Saki Bottle Only...$35.00 – 40.00
9th, Brown Teapot ....$12.50 – 15.00

Page 104

Top Row:
Toby Pitcher, barkeep holding two mugs 4⅞"..............$35.00 – 45.00
Steins, three musketeers partying ....$22.50 – 25.00
Winker Pitcher ....$17.50 – 20.00

2nd Row:
Toby w/Mustache..$30.00 – 32.50

Individual Teapot, 3⅝" ....$35.00 – 37.50
Toby Pitcher, 4⅞" ....$40.00 – 50.00

3rd Row:
Stein, Man and Woman w/Dog, 8½" ....$35.00 – 40.00
Mug w/Coach Scene ....$12.50 – 15.00
Stein ....$35.00 – 40.00

4th Row:
Mug w/Fishermen ....$12.50 – 15.00
Pitcher, 3" ....$15.00 – 17.50
Pitcher, 2" ....$12.50 – 15.00
Pitcher ....$20.00 – 22.50
Pitcher ....$20.00 – 22.50

Page 106

Top Row:
1st, "Clever Bear" ....$45.00 – 55.00
2nd and 3rd, "Walking Bear"...............................$40.00 – 50.00 ea.

2nd Row:
1st, "Roll Over Cat"...$40.00 – 50.00
2nd, "Playful Cat" ....$25.00 – 35.00
3rd – 5th, Walking Bears ....$40.00 – 50.00

3rd Row:
"X Car," Lady driver..$90.00 – 100.00
"Walking Goat" ....$45.00 – 55.00
"Baby Tortoise" ....$40.00 – 50.00

4th Row:
"Circus Elephant" ....$95.00 – 110.00
"Elephant on Barrel"..$300.00 – 350.00

5th Row:
"Dancing Couple"...$40.00 – 50.00
Smaller Dancing Couple ....$30.00 – 40.00
"Jumping Dog" ....$20.00 – 25.00

Page 108

Top Row:
Horn ....$25.00 – 30.00
Alligator Clickers...$40.00 – 45.00 dz.
Composition Doll..$30.00 – 35.00
Silver-haired Doll...$22.50 – 25.00
Microscope..$85.00 – 100.00
Beetle Clicker in front of box ....$5.00 – 6.00

2nd Row:
Dionne Quints ....$85.00 – 100.00
Celluloid Monkey Car Mirror Hanger ....$22.50 – 25.00
Celluloid Monkey Car Mirror Hanger ....$12.50 – 15.00
Box of Eight Bisque Dolls ....$100.00 – 125.00

3rd Row:
1st and 2nd, Cameras ....$10.00 – 12.50 ea.
3rd, Mouse ....$7.50 – 10.00
4th, Rabbit, hanging ....$7.50 – 10.00
5th, Harmonica ....$15.00 – 17.50
6th, Harmonicas ....$15.00 – 17.50
7th, Harmonica ....$15.00 – 17.50
8th and 9th, Compasses..$17.50 – 20.00 ea.

4th Row:
"Special Police" Badge ....$12.50 – 15.00
Piano Baby ....$75.00 – 90.00
"Meyi Grand" on top ....$65.00 – 75.00
Mirror ....$7.50 – 10.00
Pistol ....$12.50 – 15.00
Ukulele..$40.00 – 50.00
Water Pistol, bird embossed on side ....$6.00 – 8.00

5th Row:
Badminton Shuttlecock...$8.00 – 10.00
Doll in Basket ....$30.00 – 35.00
Black Doll ....$45.00 – 50.00
Pair Black Dolls ....$60.00 – 75.00
Baby..$30.00 – 35.00
Ping Pong Ball ....$12.50 – 15.00
Small Composition Doll ....$22.50 – 25.00
Snow Baby w/Seal ....$35.00 – 40.00

Page 110

Top Row:
Vase, 3¾", embossed yellow rose.............................$17.50 – 20.00
Vase, 3⅜", blue floral ....$17.50 – 20.00
Vase, 5⅞", blue w/gold handles...............................$22.50 – 25.00
Vase, pink w/embossed blue rose ....$20.00 – 22.50
Vase, 6", urn style ....$20.00 – 22.50
Vase, 6¼", urn style ....$22.50 – 25.00
Vase, white blossoms ....$12.50 – 15.00
Vase, green with floral scene ....$8.00 – 10.00
Vase, yellow and blue stripe ....$12.50 – 15.00
Vase, green w/embossed red rose ....$25.00 – 30.00

2nd Row:
1st and 2nd, Vases, 4¼", green w/embossed rose........$15.00 – 17.50 ea.
3rd, 4th, and 8th, Vases, green, blue, or white w/embossed
    flowers...$7.50 – 10.00 ea.
5th and 6th, Vases, yellow w/embossed flowers ....$10.00 – 12.50 ea.
7th, Vase, rose w/lace ....$15.00 – 17.50
9th, Vase, pink w/white roses ....$7.50 – 10.00
10th – 13th, Vases, orange or white w/flowers..............$4.00 – 5.00 ea.

3rd Row:
1st and 2nd, Vases, "Wedgwood-like" ....$7.50 – 10.00 ea.
3rd, Vase, 1¾", pink, fluted top ....$5.00 – 6.00
4th and 11th, Vases, 2", white ....$2.50 – 4.00 ea.
5th, Vase, 1⅞", gold handles ....$2.00 – 3.00
6th, Vase, pink w/embossed flowers........................$5.00 – 6.00
7th, Vase, brown w/roses ....$4.00 – 5.00
8th, Vase, 3½"...$12.50 – 15.00
9th and 10th, Vases ....$7.50 – 10.00 ea.
12th, Vase, green w/white spots ....$8.00 – 10.00
13th and 14th, Vases, 3⅝" ....$10.00 – 12.50 ea.

4th Row:
1st, 9th, and 10th, Vases, 4¼"..................................$12.50 – 15.00 ea.
2nd, Vase, 4¼"...$12.50 – 15.00
3rd and 5th, Vases, white floral ....$5.00 – 6.00 ea.
4th, Vase ....$2.00 – 3.00
6th, Vase, two handled floral ....$4.00 – 5.00
7th, Vase, pear shaped ....$12.50 – 15.00
8th, Vase, garden scene ....$10.00 – 12.50
11th, Vase, Iris ....$10.00 – 12.50

5th Row:

1st, Vase, 3½", orange flower ....$10.00 – 12.50
2nd, Vase, 3⅝", berries ....$10.00 – 12.50
3rd, Vase, pink corn ....$15.00 – 17.50
4th, Vase, floral ....$10.00 – 12.50
5th, Vase, blue w/red tulip ....$10.00 – 12.50
6th, Vase, cornucopia ....$10.00 – 12.50
7th, Vase, pagoda scene ....$15.00 – 17.50
8th and 9th, Vases, embossed dragons.....................$15.00 – 17.50 ea.
10th, Vase, green w/flowers......................................$7.50 – 10.00
11th, Vase, carriage scene ....$6.00 – 8.00

Page 112

Top Row:

1st, Colonial Lady w/Fan, 12" ....$75.00 – 85.00
2nd, Bisque Clock w/Angels, 11¼" ....$550.00 – 600.00
3rd, Colonial Man to match 1st Lady, 12" ....$75.00 – 85.00
1st and 3rd Pair ....$200.00 – 225.00

2nd Row:

Vase, 11¼", scenic view ....$90.00 – 100.00
Oriental Dancer, 14¼" ....$100.00 – 125.00
Lady w/Sideways Collar, 10⅛" ....$50.00 – 60.00

Page 114

Top photograph:

Mikky phonograph, 4½" x 5¾" x 4" ....$150.00 – 200.00
Wool hooked rug, 3' x 5' ....$75.00 – 100.00

Page 116

Book..$65.00 – 75.00

Page 118

Bottom page

Boy, 9", "Florence" look-a-like ....$35.00 – 40.00
Girl Mate, 8¼", same marks ....$35.00 – 40.00

Page 119

1st, Fly Swatter ....$22.50 – 25.00
2nd, Fly Rod in Box ....$50.00 – 60.00

Page 120

Top Row:

Coach, 6" x 9" ....$150.00 – 200.00
Man Holding Flowers, 10½" ....$75.00 – 85.00
Seated Lady w/Book, 6" ....$40.00 – 45.00

2nd Row:

Seated Lady ....$80.00 – 90.00
Standing Lady ....$100.00 – 115.00
Standing w/Golden Lace ....$80.00 – 90.00
Standing Lady w/Crinoline Skirt ....$50.00 – 60.00
Mate to 4th ....$50.00 – 60.00

3rd Row:

Cupid Holding Shell ....$30.00 – 35.00
Cupid Blowing Horn ....$75.00 – 90.00
Angel ....$35.00 – 40.00
4th and 5th, Babies Riding Butterfly ....$17.50 – 20.00 ea.

4th Row:

Cupid-type Kid..$22.50 – 25.00
Cupid-type Kid..$22.50 – 25.00
Cupid-type Kid..$22.50 – 25.00
"Hummel"-type Boy ....$30.00 – 35.00
Oriental Boy ....$10.00 – 12.50
Black Boy w/Dice ....$30.00 – 35.00
Girl w/Dog ....$20.00 – 25.00

Page 122

Top Row:

Cow Creamer ....$35.00 – 40.00
Parrot Planter ....$35.00 – 40.00
Bird Planter ....$15.00 – 17.50
Nude Handled Mug ....$25.00 – 30.00

2nd Row:

1st and 2nd, Mart & George Salt & Pepper Shakers ...$17.50 – 20.00 pr.
3rd, Cat and Birds Cage on Tree Shakers ....$20.00 – 25.00 set
4th, Oriental Carrying Basket Shakers.......................$22.50 – 25.00 set
5th, Flowering Cabbage Shakers on Stand ....$15.00 – 17.50 set

3rd Row:

1st, "Walking Small Bear" ....$40.00 – 50.00
2nd and 3rd, Cats ....$5.00 – 6.00
4th, Parrot Car Swinger ....$7.50 – 10.00
5th – 7th, Birds..$6.00 – 8.00 ea.
8th, Barber "Blades" Disposal in Head......................$40.00 – 50.00

4th Row:

Cigarette Box w/Horse Scene ....$15.00 – 17.50
Ash Tray for above box ....$2.50 – 4.00 ea.
Metal Lighter ....$12.50 – 15.00
Small Lighter ....$6.00 – 8.00
Mouse..$7.50 – 10.00
Rose Embossed Bowl and Cover...............................$25.00 – 30.00

Page 124

Left foreground:

Couple at Piano, 5½" ....$50.00 – 65.00
Bisque Piano Baby...$75.00 – 90.00

Left background:

Bisque Clock w/Angels, 11¼" ....$550.00 – 650.00

Center foreground:

Lacquerware Basket w/Metal Handle ....$55.00 – 65.00

Center background:

Oriental Dancer, 14¼" ....$100.00 – 125.00

Right foreground:

Lady w/Children on Embossed Floral Shoe, 5"..........$75.00 – 85.00

Right background:

Horse w/Rider, 10¼" ....$150.00 – 175.00

Schroeder's ANTIQUES Price Guide

. . . is the #1 best-selling antiques & collectibles value guide on the market today, and here's why . . .

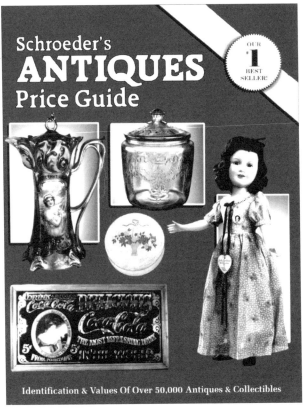

Schroeder's **ANTIQUES** Price Guide

OUR **#1** BEST SELLER!

Identification & Values Of Over 50,000 Antiques & Collectibles

8½ x 11, 608 Pages, $14.95

• *More than 300 advisors, well-known dealers, and top-notch collectors work together with our editors to bring you accurate information regarding pricing and identification.*

• *More than 45,000 items in almost 500 categories are listed along with hundreds of sharp original photos that illustrate not only the rare and unusual, but the common, popular collectibles as well.*

• *Each large close-up shot shows important details clearly. Every subject is represented with histories and background information, a feature not found in any of our competitors' publications.*

• *Our editors keep abreast of newly developing trends, often adding several new categories a year as the need arises.*

If it merits the interest of today's collector, you'll find it in *Schroeder's*. And you can feel confident that the information we publish is up to date and accurate. Our advisors thoroughly check each category to spot inconsistencies, listings that may not be entirely reflective of market dealings, and lines too vague to be of merit. Only the best of the lot remains for publication.

Without doubt, you'll find
SCHROEDER'S ANTIQUES PRICE GUIDE
the only one to buy for
reliable information and values.

COLLECTOR BOOKS
A Division of Schroeder Publishing Co., Inc.